BRISTOL'S TRAMWAYS

Series editor Robert J Harley

Peter Davey

Cover Picture - Brislington Depot and Construction Works in 1938 with cars 108, 49, and 207 as the day's "rush cars" and car 217 standing by on the Hotwells route. (S.Miles Davey)

Cover Colours - The colours used on this cover are as close as possible to the dark blue and white used latterly on the Bristol fleet. The blue is taken from a destination board in the author's collection.

FOREWORD
from Timothy West

I've always been very sentimental about trams, as I suspect many people are. The crowds thronging the Thames Embankment to say an affectionate farewell to the last of the London trams in July 1952 were the greatest I had seen since VJ Night. A line of pennies - touching each other - stretched along the line from Westminster Bridge to Blackfriars Bridge, waiting to be run over by the very last tram. My other mementoes of that evening include the buttons from the uniform of one of the conductors - a cheery Glaswegian, I remember, who, having thoughtfully been provided with a bottle of whisky, happily permitted souvenir hunting passengers to remove anything they fancied from his tram and his person.

But this book is about Bristol trams. I remember them, though they disappeared from the scene when I was a lot younger. The author and I in fact lived practically next door to each other in Redland, and the familiar noise of the No. 4 trams groaning up the incline of Redland Road is a common memory (the backs of our houses can be seen on the right in picture 26).

Peter Davey has kept, and carefully sorted through, his father's remarkable photographic study of Bristol's trams, and they form the basis of this definitive record.

I write this having, in the past week, travelled once again on trams: in Manchester and in Sheffield. Their reintroduction seems to be a great success. Maybe Bristol - never, perhaps, a city to be first off the mark, but practised at hanging back and profiting by others successes or mistakes - will eventually succumb? It would be good to hear them again ...

Timothy West
March 1995

First published August 1995

Published by Middleton Press
Easebourne Lane
Midhurst
West Sussex
GU29 9AZ
Tel: 01730 813169
Fax: 01730 812601

ISBN 1 873793 57 X

Design - Deborah Goodridge

Printed & bound by Biddles Ltd,
Guildford and Kings Lynn

CONTENTS

DEDICATION

To my father, who so loved Bristol's trams but sadly passed away before "our" book could be completed.

INTRODUCTION AND ACKNOWLEDGEMENTS

My father, S.Miles Davey, was a railway and tramway photographer in the twenties and thirties and Bristol's trams were his subjects from 1937 to 1941. From his negatives are numerous studies which I have often felt would make the basis of a book.

As 1995 is Bristol's centenary of the first electric tram, I felt this to be an appropriate time to publish the most interesting of them.

I would like to mention how grateful I am to four other photographers who have kindly let me use their photographs. These are G.Baddeley, S.G.Jackman, H.B.Priestley and the late W.A.Camwell. Also included are pictures from the M.J.Tozer collection and that of the late John Appleby. Others are acknowledged throughout the text. Special thanks to John Gillham for his superb map of the system as it was in the late 1930s. Also the same to Eric Thornton for his detailed plan of the standard Bristol tram. I wish to thank Michael Tozer for supplying so much information from the diaries of Mr Charles Challenger dated 1898 - 1922; Derek Hodgson, regarding the 203 - 232 series of cars; J.H. Price, regarding details of trucks; John Gray for various measurement details; Eddie White, who was employed as a tram body builder at Brislington on the last batch 233 - 237; the staff of the Bristol Record Office for supplying copies of the maps they hold and kindly giving me permission to reproduce them in specific sections; Norman Davey, Sir George White, David Withers, the late Keith Williams for his notes recording tramcar movements, and a special thank you to my life-long friend, Timothy West, who kindly found time to write the Foreword.

Although many plates taken by my father were featured over twenty years ago in Reece Winstone's book "Trams", I hope that the reprinting of some of them will still hold their interest. My sincere thanks to Donald Packham for his invaluable assistance in preparing and typing the text - many times!

Lastly to my wife, Teresa, who has survived being surrounded by tram memorabilia for so many years.

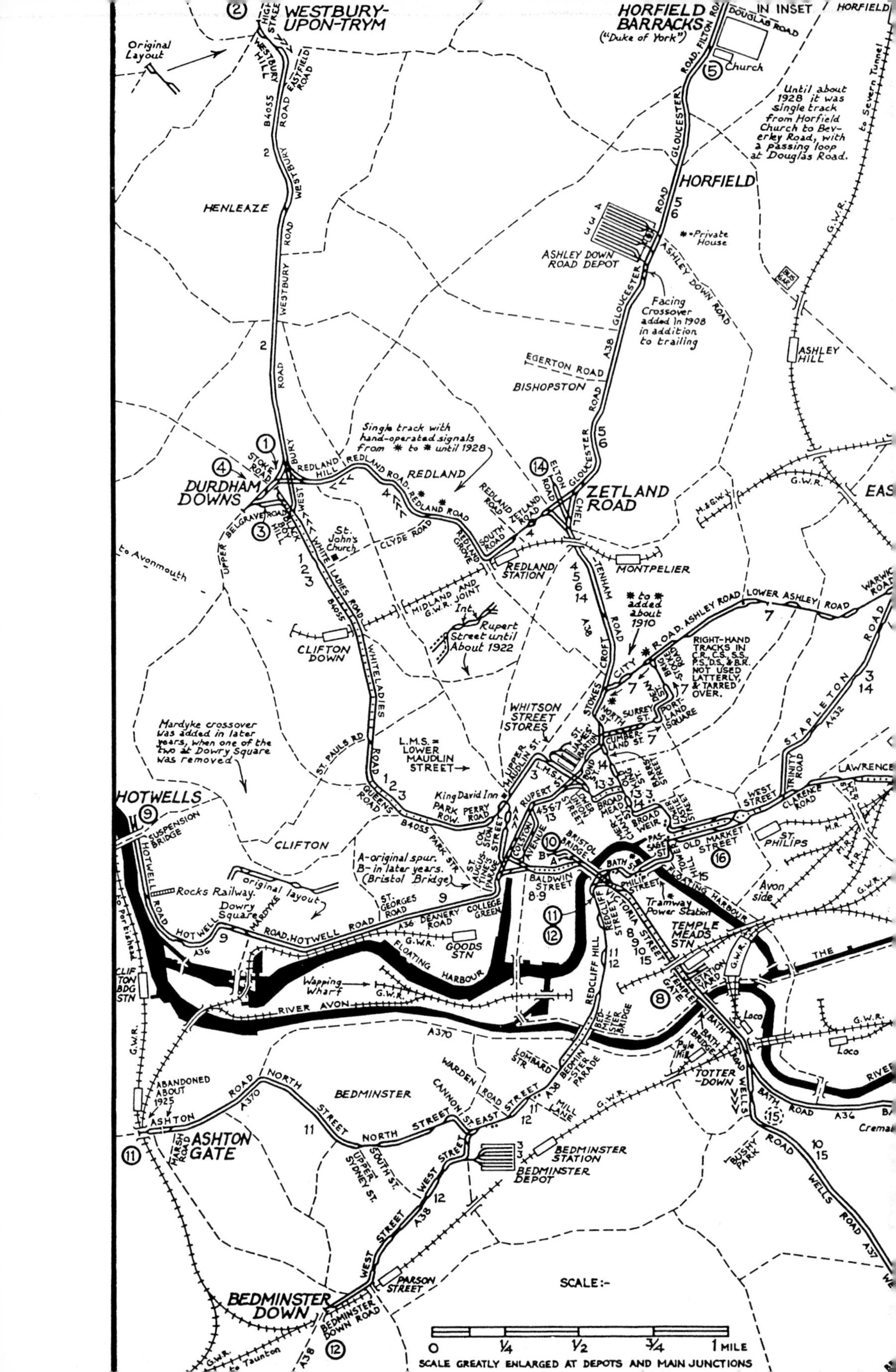

WESTBURY-UPON-TRYM
HIGH STREET
Original Layout
WESTBURY HILL
EASTFIELD ROAD
B4055
WESTBURY ROAD
HENLEAZE
HORFIELD BARRACKS
("Duke of York")
IN INSET
HORFIELD
DOUGLAS ROAD
Church
FILTON ROAD
GLOUCESTER ROAD
Until about 1928 it was single track from Horfield Church to Beverley Road, with a passing loop at Douglas Road.
to Severn Tunnel
HORFIELD
G.W.R.
* Private House
ASHLEY DOWN ROAD DEPOT
ASHLEY DOWN ROAD
Facing Crossover added in 1908 in addition to trailing
A38
EGERTON ROAD
BISHOPSTON
ASHLEY HILL
Single track with hand-operated signals from * to * until 1928
DURDHAM DOWNS
STOKE ROAD
REDLAND HILL
REDLAND ROAD
REDLAND
BELGRAVE ROAD
BLACKBOY HILL
WHITE LADIES ROAD
St. John's Church
CLYDE ROAD
REDLAND GROVE
SOUTH ROAD
ZETLAND ROAD
ELTON ROAD
ZETLAND ROAD
CHELTENHAM ROAD
M.&G.W.
G.W.R.
EAS
REDLAND STATION
MONTPELIER
to Avonmouth
UPPER BELGRAVE ROAD
MIDLAND AND G.W.R. JOINT
Int. Rupert Street until About 1922
* to * added about 1910
CLIFTON DOWN
WHITELADIES ROAD
CITY ROAD
ASHLEY ROAD
LOWER ASHLEY ROAD
WARWICK ROAD
RIGHT-HAND TRACKS IN C.R., C.S., S.S., P.S., D.S., & B.R. NOT USED LATTERLY, & TARRED OVER.
BRIGSTOCKE ROAD
STOKES CROFT
NORTH ST.
SURREY ST.
PORTLAND SQUARE
CUMBERLAND ST.
STAPLETON ROAD
A432
TRINITY ROAD
Mardyke crossover was added in later years, when one of the two at Dowry Square was removed
WHITSON STREET STORES
L.M.S. = LOWER MAUDLIN STREET
UPPER MAUDLIN ST.
ST. JAMES' BARTON
L.M.S.
RUPERT ST.
BOND ST.
OLD KING ST.
BARRS STREET
ST. PAULS RD
QUEENS ROAD
King David Inn
PARK ROW
PERRY ROAD
LOWER UNION STREET
BROADMEAD
BROAD WEIR
LOWER CASTLE STREET
WEST STREET
CLARENCE ROAD
LAWRENCE
HOTWELLS
SUSPENSION BRIDGE
CLIFTON
COLSTON STREET
COLSTON AVENUE
BRISTOL BRIDGE
PASSAGE ST.
OLD MARKET STREET
TOWER HILL
ST. PHILIPS
M.R.
A-original spur. B-in later years. (Bristol Bridge)
ST. AUGUSTINES PARADE
PARK STR
BALDWIN STREET
BATH ST.
PHILIP STREET
Avon side
HOTWELL ROAD
Rocks Railway.
original layout
Dowry Square
MARDYKE
ST. GEORGES ROAD
DEANERY ROAD
COLLEGE GREEN
REDCLIFF HILL
VICTORIA STREET
Tramway Power Station
FLOATING HARBOUR
TEMPLE MEADS STN
to Portishead
A36
HOTWELL ROAD
G.W.R.
GOODS STN
FLOATING HARBOUR
THE
CLIFTON BDG STN
Wapping Wharf
G.W.R.
STATION YARD
TEMPLE GATE
RIVER AVON
BEDMINSTER BRIDGE
Loco
G.W.R.
A370
BATH ROAD
Pyle Hill
BATH BRIDGE
Loco
LOMBARD STR
WARDEN ROAD
BEDMINSTER PARADE
TOTTERDOWN
RIVER
G.W.R.
ABANDONED ABOUT 1925
ASHTON ROAD
NORTH STREET
BEDMINSTER
CANNON ST.
EAST STREET
A38
MILL LANE
G.W.R.
WELLS ROAD
BATH ROAD
A36
Cremat
ASHTON GATE
MARSH ROAD
NORTH STREET
UPPER SIDNEY ST.
SOUTH ST.
WEST STREET
BEDMINSTER STATION
BEDMINSTER DEPOT
BUSHY PARK
WELLS ROAD
A37
WEST STREET
A38
PARSON STREET
SCALE:-
BEDMINSTER DOWN
BEDMINSTER DOWN ROAD
G.W.R. to Taunton
A38
0 1/4 1/2 3/4 1 MILE
SCALE GREATLY ENLARGED AT DEPOTS AND MAIN JUNCTIONS

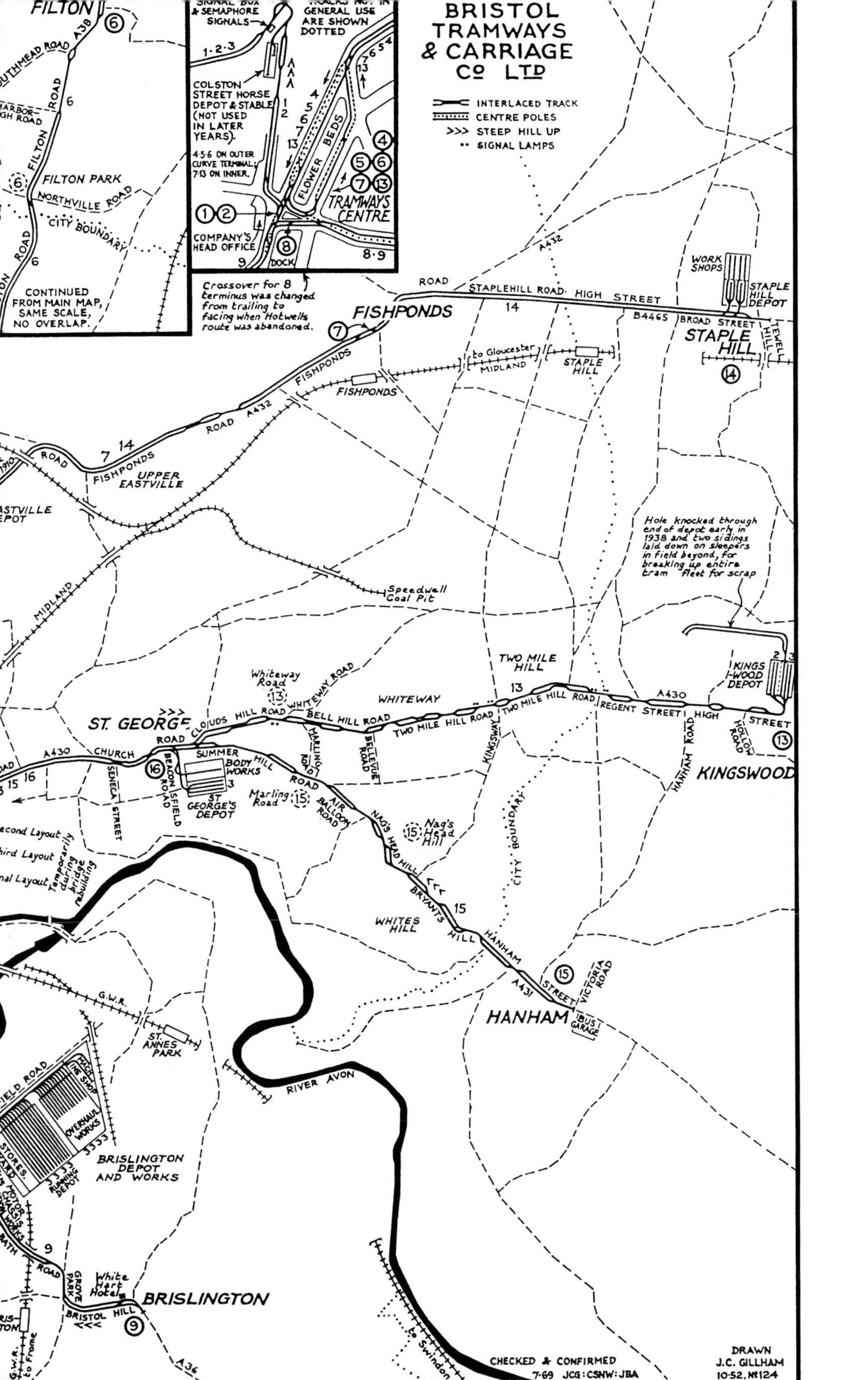
BRISTOL TRAMWAYS & CARRIAGE Co LTD
INTERLACED TRACK
CENTRE POLES
STEEP HILL UP
SIGNAL LAMPS
FILTON
SOUTHMEAD ROAD
FILTON ROAD
FILTON PARK
NORTHVILLE ROAD
CITY BOUNDARY
CONTINUED FROM MAIN MAP, SAME SCALE, NO OVERLAP.
SIGNAL BOX & SEMAPHORE SIGNALS
COLSTON STREET HORSE DEPOT & STABLE (NOT USED IN LATER YEARS).
4·5·6 ON OUTER CURVE TERMINAL; 7·13 ON INNER.
COMPANY'S HEAD OFFICE
FLOWER BEDS
TRAMWAYS CENTRE
GENERAL USE ARE SHOWN DOTTED
DOCK
Crossover for 8 terminus was changed from trailing to facing when Hotwells route was abandoned.
FISHPONDS
STAPLEHILL ROAD · HIGH STREET
WORK SHOPS
STAPLE HILL DEPOT
B4465
BROAD STREET
STAPLE HILL
TEWELL HILL
to Gloucester
MIDLAND
FISHPONDS ROAD
UPPER EASTVILLE
EASTVILLE DEPOT
Speedwell Coal Pit
Hole knocked through end of depot early in 1938 and two sidings laid down on sleepers in field beyond, for breaking up entire tram fleet for scrap
KINGS-WOOD DEPOT
TWO MILE HILL
Whiteway Road
WHITEWAY ROAD
WHITEWAY
ST. GEORGE
CLOUDS HILL ROAD
BELL HILL ROAD
TWO MILE HILL ROAD
REGENT STREET
HIGH STREET
A430
HOLLOW ROAD
HANHAM ROAD
KINGSWOOD
KINGSWAY
BELLEVUE ROAD
MARLING ROAD
CHURCH ROAD
SENECA STREET
BEACONSFIELD ROAD
SUMMER HILL ROAD
BODY WORKS
ST GEORGE'S DEPOT
Marling Road
AIR BALLOON ROAD
NAG'S HEAD HILL
Nag's Head Hill
CITY BOUNDARY
Second Layout
Third Layout
Final Layout
Temporarily during bridge rebuilding
BRYANTS HILL
WHITES HILL
HANHAM STREET
A431
VICTORIA ROAD
HANHAM
BUS GARAGE
G.W.R.
ST. ANNES PARK
RIVER AVON
FIELD ROAD
MACH. SHOP
OVERHAUL WORKS
STORES
RUNNING DEPOT
BRISLINGTON DEPOT AND WORKS
BATH ROAD
GROVE PARK
White Hart Hotel
BRISLINGTON
BRISTOL HILL
G.W.R. to Frome
A36
to Swindon
CHECKED & CONFIRMED 7·69 JCG:CSNW:JBA
DRAWN J.C. GILLHAM 10·52. No124

GEOGRAPHICAL SETTING

Bristol, at present, is in the County of Avon which was formed from parts of Gloucestershire and Somerset. It is situated on the rivers Avon and Froom (Frome) and the two together wind their way through the gorge, under Brunel's Suspension Bridge, to Avonmouth before joining the Severn. A few remnants of Roman construction can be found in the City as well as some interesting evidence of tramway operation.

The Ordnance Survey maps are to the scale of 25" to the mile (1:2500) and date from 1903 to 1913.

Horse tram routes

Drawbridge - Perry Road - Redland (Apsley Road)
Drawbridge - Horfield Depot
Drawbridge - Cumberland Street - Ashley Road - Warwick Road
Hotwells (Dowry Square) - Drawbridge - Joint Station
Bristol Bridge (Redcliffe Street) - Ashton Gate (Coronation Road)
Bristol Bridge (Redcliffe Street) - Bedminster
Old Market - Bath Street - Joint Station - Totterdown - Arno's Vale
Old Market - Perry Road - Redland (Apsley Road)
Old Market - Eastville
Old Market - St. George - Kingswood
"Drawbridge" was later discontinued and "Tramways Centre" substituted.

Electric tram routes

The routes were not numbered until November 1913 and were as follows -

1 Tramways Centre - Whiteladies Road - Durdham Downs
2 Tramways Centre - Whiteladies Road - Durdham Downs - Westbury
3 Eastville - Old Market - Whiteladies Road - Durdham Downs
4 Tramways Centre - Zetland Road - Durdham Downs
5 Tramways Centre - Ashley Down Road - Horfield Barracks
6 Tramways Centre - Ashley Down Road - Horfield Barracks - Filton Park - Filton
7 Tramways Centre - Warwick Road - Eastville - Fishponds
8 Tramways Centre - Temple Meads Station
9 Hotwells - Tramways Centre - Temple Meads Station - Arno's Vale - Depot - Brislington
10 Bristol Bridge - Knowle
11 Bristol Bridge - Ashton Road
12 Bristol Bridge - Bedminster Depot - Bedminster Down
13 Tramways Centre - Old Market - St. George - Whiteway Rd - Kingswood
14 Zetland Road - Old Market - Eastville - Fishponds - Staple Hill
15 Knowle - Bushy Park - Old Market - St. George - Marling Road - Nags Head Hill - Hanham
16 Old Market - St George
17 Hotwells - Tramways Centre - Temple Meads Station

Route 1 was withdrawn and absorbed into 2.
Route 8 was withdrawn and absorbed into 9.
Route 13 for a while, did not run to the Tramways Centre but terminated at Old Market.
Route 16. was a "rush hour" route only and was absorbed into 13 and 15.
Route 17 ran to meet the Campbell's steamers and was withdrawn at the same time as route 8.

Trams did not actually run along Ashley Down Rd., Marling Rd., or Whiteway Road, and route 14 did not enter Zetland Rd.

From 1902 to 1905, the route from Hanham, having reached Old Market, was extended to the Tramways Centre.

HISTORICAL BACKGROUND

Bristol's foundation is probably lost in the mists of time, possibly founded by a Welsh King Dyfneval and his son Brennus or Bryn.

In 1373, the town of Bristol was granted a Charter by Edward III thus making it a County in itself. On creation of a Bishopric in 1542, it then became a City, and the abbey church of the monastery of St. Augustine became the Cathedral.

The first trams were pulled by horses and commenced on 9th August 1875 running from Perry Road (Colston Curve) to Apsley Road, known as Redland Terminus. The horses were kept at the Colston Stables, wedged between the triangle of Perry Road, Colston Street and Griffin Lane (now Lower Park Row).

On 14th October 1895, the first electric cars ran from Old Market to Kingswood and were kept at the depot in Beaconsfield Road, St. George, which was also the power station.

Eventually 17 tram routes existed which were reduced to 12 in the final pattern. (The first bus route was 18).

In 1900/01 the largest depot, workshop and maintenance complex was built at Brislington and it was used for the construction of trams. Later many of the City's buses were built and housed there. It still exists (a listed building) and some of the tram tracks are still down in the old engineering shops at the far end.

The fleet commenced with various horse trailers, totalling 109 with 678 horses. These were eventually replaced by electric cars which totalled 237. The last new batch was built in 1920 to the same basic open top design and style as those of twenty years before. With a few exceptions all cars were rebuilt as the "standard" car through the 1920s and 1930s.

Abandonment commenced in 1938 and was to be carried out in five phases, but during an air raid on Good Friday 1941, bombs dropped on St Philip's Bridge outside the power station and disrupted the system's electricity supply. Buses immediately appeared, unplanned, the next morning. During the next few weeks the powerless cars had to be towed to Kingswood to face their sad cremation. The last one to disappear in the flames was car 64 on 16th October 1941.

TRAM CAR SERVICES

		WEEKDAYS.		SUNDAYS.	
		First dep. A.M.	Last dep. P.M.	First dep. P.M.	Last dep. P.M.
Service No. 2	**T. Centre, D. Down & Westbury**				
	From T. Centre to Westbury	5 30	1055	2 20	10 0
	,, T. Centre to D. Down	5 30	1120	2 20	1020
	,, D. Down to Westbury	5 35	1110	2 20	1015
	,, Westbury to T. Centre	5 45	11 0	2 35	10 5
	,, Westbury to D. Down	5 45	1125	2 35	1030
	,, D. Down to T. Centre	5 50	1110	2 20	1020
Service No. 3	**D. Down, Old Market & Eastville**				
	From Eastville to Old Market	5 20	1120	2 0	1030
	,, Eastville to D. Downs	5 20	1045	2 0	9 40
	,, Old Market to D. Down	5 35	11 0	2 10	1010
	,, Old Market to Eastville	5 30	1140	2 15	1040
	,, D. Down to Old Mkt. & Eastville	6 20	1120	2 35	1015
Service No. 4	**D. Down & T. Centre (via Zetland Road)**				
	From T. Centre to D. Down	6 30	1110	2 25	1015
	,, D. Down to T. Centre	7 0	1110	2 30	10 0
	,, D. Down to Zetland Road	7 0	1130	2 30	1040
Services No. 5-6	**T. Centre, Horfield & Filton**				
	From Ashley Down Rd. to T. Centre	5 0	1110	2 0	1020
	,, T. Centre to Filton	5 20	1110	2 25	1010
	,, Filton to T. Centre	5 25	11 0	2 10	1010
	,, Filton to Ashley Down Road	5 25	1140	2 10	1040
	,, T. Centre to Horfield Barracks.	5 20	1120	2 26	1025
Service No. 7	**T. Centre & Fishponds**				
	From Fishponds to T. Centre	4 55	1045	2 0	10 5
	,, Warwick Road to T. Centre	5 10	11 0	2 5	1015
	,, T. Centre to Fishponds	5 30	1115	2 30	1020
Services No. 8-9	**Hotwells & Brislington**				
	From Brislington to Hotwells	5 25	1050	2 10	1025
	,, Brislington to T. Centre	5 25	1120	2 10	1025
	,, Hotwells to T. Centre	5 35	1125	2 25	11 0
	,, T. Centre to Brislington	5 35	1130	2 15	1030
	,, Hotwells to Brislington	5 35	1120	2 25	1015
	,, T. Centre to Joint Station	5 35	1140	2 15	1110
	,, Joint Station to T. Centre	5 10	1130	2 5	1040
Service No. 10	**Bristol Bridge & Knowle**				
	From Knowle	5 25	1125	2 20	1025
	Bristol Bridge	5 40	1140	2 15	1020

The Bristol Tramways & Carriage Co., Ltd.

SPECIAL INSTRUCTIONS TO DRIVERS AND ALL CONCERNED.

To guard against improper working resulting in an excessive maximum output of electric current, the following conditions as to working are laid down as supplementary to the Rules and Regulations, and must be strictly observed by Drivers.

INTERVAL BETWEEN CARS.

No car must approach a preceding car nearer than 80 yards except at Junctions and at Termini. At Junctions the main line car must have right of way, when the other car or cars must be brought to a standstill and wait until the above named space intervenes before again moving on.

On a straight line the distance between two posts is 40 yards, therefore 80 yards would include three posts.

The above intervening space must be observed on level lines and moderate grades.

ON STEEP GRADES.

On the following steep grades two up cars must not be ascending, nor two down cars be descending at the same time between :—

Knowle : Bushy Park and Holy Nativity.
Knowle : Sydenham Road and Somerset Road.
Redcliff Hill : by Redcliff Church.
Infirmary Hill : Whitsun Street and top of curve.
Blackboy Hill : Wellington Park and Worrall Road.
Redland Green Hill, Clyde Road and Redland Green.
Gloucester Road : Brynland Avenue and Hatherly Rd.
Church Road : Northcote Road and Fountain.
Air Balloon Hill : Top of Hill and Trooper's Hill Road.
Nag's Head Hill : Trooper's Hill Road and Top of Hill.
Bryant's Hill : Rag Factory Lane and Top of Hill.
College Green Hill : Denmark Street and Royal Hotel.
Redland Hill : only one car at a time must occupy the lines between Manor Park and Grove Road.

LOSING CURRENT:

From Power House.

If at any time the current is cut off, cars on down grades must stop as soon as the fact becomes known. This is shown at night by the lights going out, and by day by the stopping of other cars on the up grade. Put driving handle to " off " at once. The cars must not be moved again until the current returns. Turn on the light circuit on coming to a standstill, daylight or dark. The lights will return when current is again switched on.

From Canopy Switch.

If the automatic switch under the canopy of the car opens, it indicates that something is wrong with the car. Put the controller at once to " off " position. Then replace the canopy switch. If on attempting to start the car a second and a third time, and if the switch opens after the third attempt, leave the switch out and have the disabled car drawn back to the depot by another car.

STARTING AFTER LOSS OF CURRENT FROM POWER HOUSE.

As soon as Current returns as shewn by the Lighted Lamps.

START CARS AT ONCE BETWEEN :—

Tramways Centre and Durdham Downs, No. 1.
Old Market Street and Durdham Downs.
Brislington, Joint Station and Hotwells.
Old Market and Knowle.
Statue and Knowle.

START CARS IN HALF-MINUTE (Count 30) :

Tramways Centre and Warwick Road.
Tramways Centre and Horfield.
Tramways Centre and Durdham Downs, No. 2.

START CARS IN ONE MINUTE (Count 60) :

Bristol Bridge and Bedminster Lines.

In all cases when several cars are at a standstill in sight of each other, the foremost car starts first, the others following in succeeding order.

On the old cars K2, and K10, there are nine points on the controller, the 4th, 5th, 8th and 9th being driving points. On cars B, 18, those with electric and track brake, there are eight points, the 4th and 8th being driving points, and on the cars with No. 5915 controllers, there are seven driving points and five electric brake points. The old cars, the first five points, the motors are in series, the last four in parallel. The new cars, the first four points, the motors are in series, the others in parallel.

As to proper manipulation of driving and reversing handles observe Rules 36 and 37.

Don't let the car run back when about to start.

Don't keep the brake on while passing over a curve, except on a down grade.

When about to stop, shut off current in good time, and allow the car to " drift " to stopping place.

Don't reach the terminus before time. Start punctually.

Don't stop on an up grade, if a level line is near.

PROPER USE OF BRAKES.

The track brake is to be applied on entering all very steep down grades, and kept in action by means of the catch. Apply with sufficient pressure to retard, but not to stop the car.

The speed of the car with B. 18 and No. 5915 controllers should then be regulated by the electric brake, moving the driving handle round quickly, immediately upon entering the hill to the brake-power point required to keep the car going at slow speed.

The electric brake will stop the car, but will not keep it stationary.

The electric brake **will act** with trolley on or off the wire.

Enter all down grades slowly ; the steeper the hill the slower must be the speed.

Don't use the track brake on a sharp curve.

Should the Electric Brake fail to stop the car or to control it, act as follows :—

1st Leave the electric brake on, then
2nd Apply the wheel brake and secure it with catch, then
3rd Apply track brake with both hands.

In this event use sand freely.

When going up a steep grade and the car stops, or has to be stopped, hold it stationary by means of the wheel brake ; **but should the car commence to run back,** act as follows :—

1st Apply the wheel brake, but not tightly enough to skid the wheels, and secure with catch.
2nd Apply the track brake with both hands, then
3rd Apply the electric brake, **but see that the reversing handle is in the backing position.**

In the event of a car running back the conductor must at once assist in applying the track brake and use sand freely from the rear end of the car.

When necessary for any purpose to back a car up a grade, see that the reversing handle is put in the forward position before again starting forward. If this is not done the electric brake will not act ; that is to say, **the electric brake is not effective unless the reversing handle points in the direction in which the car is travelling.**

TWO BRAKES AT ONE TIME.

The electric and the track brakes will act together.
The track and the wheel brakes will act together.

CHARLES CHALLENGER, Manager.

TRAMWAYS CENTRE, December, 1914.

Opening of the Electric Tramways

1. A few days before the Old Market - St. George - Kingswood Electric Line was opened, cars 89 and 92 are seen just delivered from Milnes, Birkenhead. The scene is at St. George and no doubt various tests are being carried out. Car 92 has yet to be fitted with her lamps, but she illustrates the seeming awkwardness of the Dick, Kerr trolley masts. (M.J.Tozer Coll.)

2. 14th October 1895, the day of the opening, has brought the crowds into Old Market Street to see a line up of 8 new cars, of the 86 - 97 series, start on the great procession up to St. George and Kingswood. Car 89 pulls off to the right, to be followed by car 92, showing letter H. For this day they were lettered A to H. (Author's Coll.)

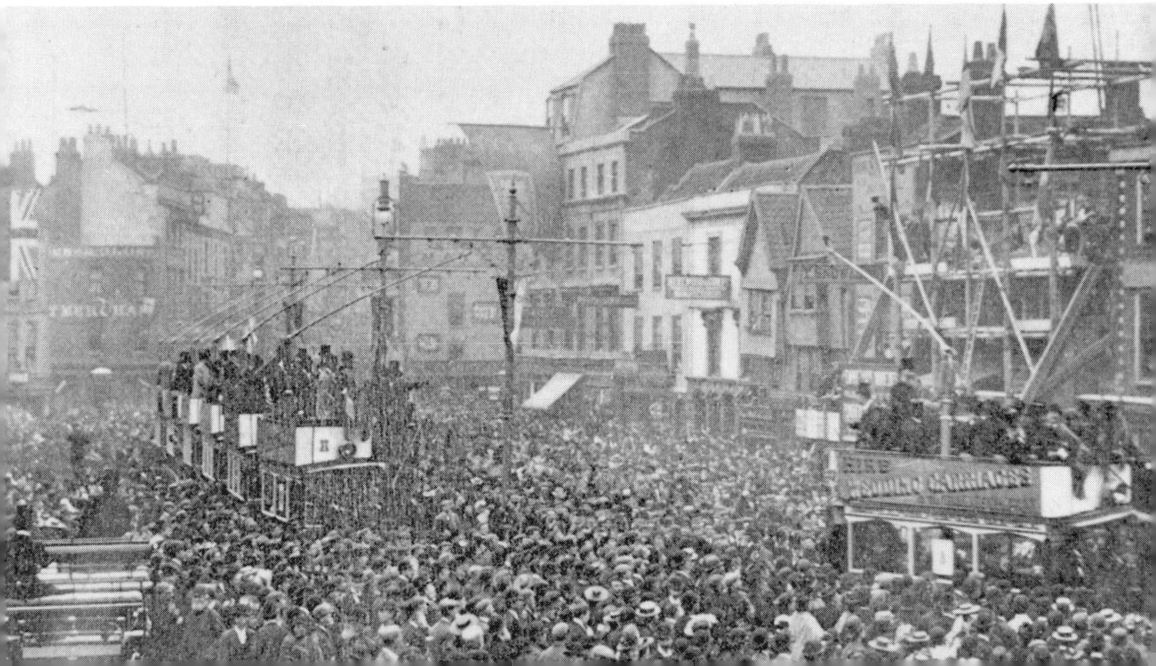

Tramways Centre - Westbury

←

3. Car 7 on the experimental Peckham P35 truck has just arrived at the west side of the Tramways Centre Triangle. This was the busy terminus for eight routes and passengers using any of them would have had to cross the roads and fight the traffic!
(Memories, Corn Exchange, Bristol)

←

4. Car 1 climbs up Colston Street from the Tramways Centre passing The Griffin Hotel. She advertises Newbery's Furnishings.
(Newham Library Service)

5. At the top of Colston Street is the great Colston Curve junction which required a set of 4 signals and a signal box. This view is taken from the roof of the Colston Stables which used to accommodate 64 horses. The signal box was opened on 17th November 1902.
(P.R.Clare)

NORTH STREET
BARR'S STREET
ST JAMES'S BARTON
BARTON STREET
HORSE FAIR
BROAD
ST. JAMES'S CHURCHYARD
HAY MARKET
BOND STREET
LOWER UNION STREET
Chapel
SILVER STREET
Police & Fire Brigade Sta.
Tramway Depot
Confectionery Works
Waiting Rooms
Brewery
WHITSON STREET
LOWER MAUDLIN STREET
MEAD
LEWINS
MONTAGUE STREET
MARLBOROUGH STREET
CHARLES STREET
Eye Hospital
More Ch.
UPPER MAUDLIN STREET
Burl. Gd.
ALFRED PARADE
MARLBOROUGH HILL
LOWER BEDFORD PLACE
TERRELL STREET
Gasometer
BLACKFRIARS
Church
ROAD

UNION STREET
DOLPHIN STREET
NELSON STREET
ALL SAINTS' STREET
St. John's Arch (Blind Gate)
TOWER LANE
JOHN STREET
TAILORS CT.
NEWMARKET PASSAGE
BROAD STREET
WINE STREET
CHEESE MARKET
MARY-LE-PORT STREET
Church
BRIDGE STREET
BACK BRIDGE STREET
HIGH STREET
CORN STREET
SMALL STREET
QUAY STREET
CHRISTMAS STREET
STONE BRIDGE
Urinal
COLSTON AVENUE
Statue
County Ct. Offices
B.M. 34·5
ST. STEPHEN'S STREET
St. Stephen's Church
ST. STEPHEN'S AVENUE
CLARE STREET
B.M. 43·4
B.M. 53·6
B.M. 40·8
BRISTOL WARD
NICHOLAS STREET
St. Nicholas's Church
FISH MARKET
BALDWIN STREET
Bank
Bristol Bridge
BRIDGE PARADE
AUGUSTINE'S BRIDGE
PARADE
Cabmen's Rest
B.M. 39·9
COLSTON STREET
HOST STREET
B.M. 74·2
B.M. 118·2

6. Car 11 negotiates the curve and is just about to cross the rails of Route 3 before joining them. There was one serious collision here on 29th January 1904. Without doubt, this is one of the most attractive photographs to include a Bristol tram. (S.G.Jackman)

7. Car 164 is climbing along a section of track being maintained in Park Row. Some unusual works vehicles are parked by the kerb. Destination states Durdham Downs via Whiteladies Road. (Author's Coll.)

8. Car 11 at the Victoria Rooms passes car 94 returning to the city. The latter is about to stop at the white brick in the foreground, locating the exact place to halt. (H.B.Priestley)

0 2708

BRISTOL TRAMWAYS AND CARRIAGE COMPANY, LTD.

Tramways Centre to Newfoundland Road, St. Nicholas Road	FARE D. 1	Horfield Ashley Down Road to Newfoundland Rd (S. Nicholas Road)
Old Market to Sussex Place (Sevier St.)	Issued subject to the Company's Regulations	Sussex (Sevier St.) to Old Market
Newfoundland Road, St. Nicholas Road, to Horfield (Ashley Down Road)		Newfoundland Road (St. Nicholas Road) to Tramways Centre
PARCEL or PACKAGE		PARCEL or PACKAGE

The Conductor is required to Punch this Ticket in the Section for which it is issued, and it must be produced or delivered up by the Passenger on demand by any Official of the Company.

[P.T.O]

9. Car 5 is at the Durdham Downs terminus in Upper Belgrave Road in about 1903 with the two crew members in the Edwardian era uniform. (Author's Coll.)

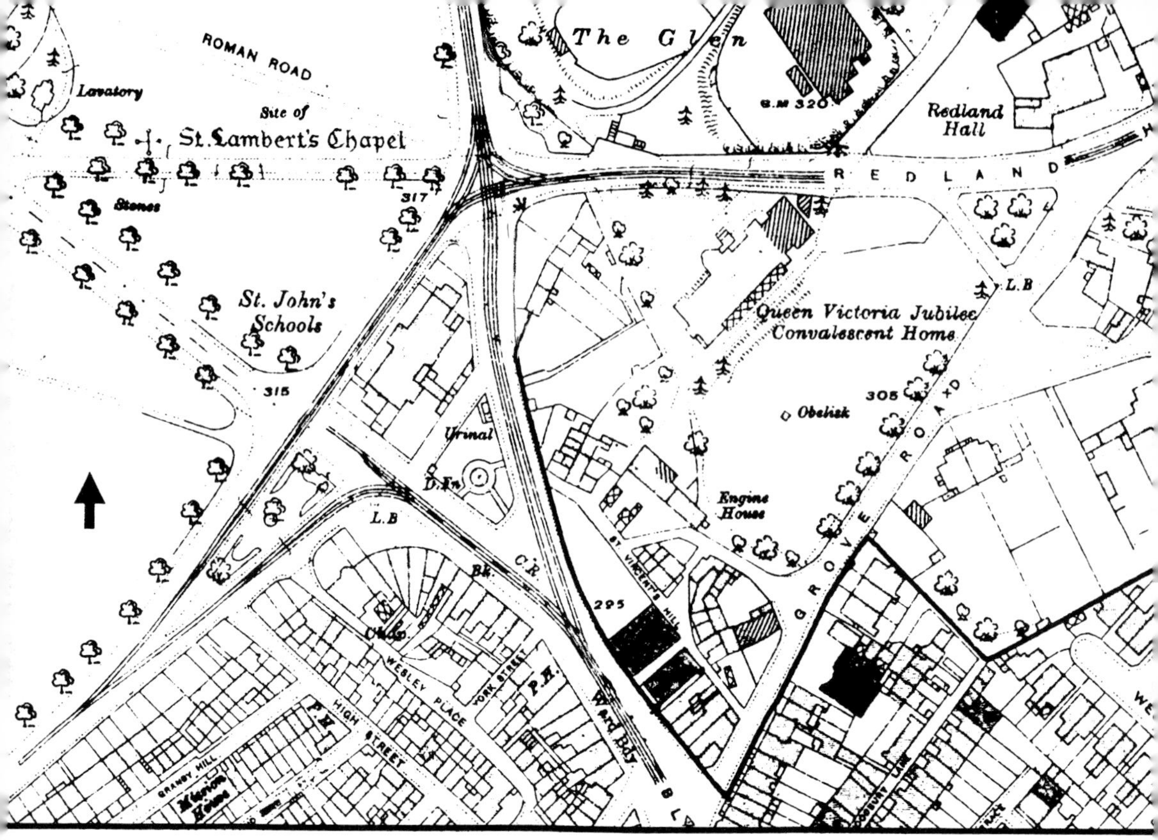

Durdham Downs terminus

10. Car 1 stands at the top of Blackboy Hill and is about to cross over to Westbury Road. She is now advertising Newbery's Furniture. This 1938 view was taken very soon before the closure of this line. (S.Miles Davey)

11. Car 94 is at the top of Westbury Hill very close to the Red Maids school. She was one of the original 86-97 series shown here since rebuilt at Brislington. (H.B.Priestley)

12. A 1938 view at the Westbury Terminus with car 5 about to leave and climb up Westbury Hill with Mr R.(Dick) Dawe at the controls. This is a good illustration of a Bristol standard car in its final condition. (S.Miles Davey)

Eastville - Durdham Downs

13. Cars 91 and 32 wait at the Terminus. Car 91 was rebuilt from the original 3 window car. She has the bold lettering on the rocker panel, whereas car 32 has the later smaller style in gold. Robertson Road is visible opposite. (W.A.Camwell)

Va 4678

BRISTOL TRAMWAYS AND CARRIAGE COMPANY, LTD.

	FARE D. 1	
Staple Hill to Fishponds (Station Rd.)		Zetland Road to Old Market
Fishponds (Station Rd.)		Old Market to Eastville
Warwick Rd Junction	Issued subject to the Company's Regulations	Warwick Rd. Junction to Fishponds (Station Rd.)
Eastville to Old Market		Fishponds (Station Rd.) to Staple Hill
Old Market to Zetland Road		
Package, Bicycle, Perambulator Parcel, etc		Package, Bicycle, Perambulator Parcel etc.

The Conductor is required to Punch this Ticket in the Section for which it is issued, and it must be produced or delivered up by the Passenger on demand by any Official of the Company. (P.T.O.

Hc 3210

BRISTOL TRAMWAYS AND CARRIAGE COMPANY, LTD.

	FARE D. 1	
Tramway Centre to Zetland Road		Durdham Downs Junction to Zetland Road
Zetland Road to Durdham Downs Junction	Issued subject to the Company's Regulations	Zetland Road to Tramways Centre.
Package, Bicycle, Perambulator Parcel, etc		Package, Bicycle, Perambulator Parcel, etc.

The Conductor is required to Punch this Ticket in the Section for which it is issued, and it must be produced or delivered up by the Passenger on demand by any Official of the Company. (P.T.O.

EASTVILLE
EMPIRE

DURDHAM DOWNS VIA
WHITELADIES ROAD
NEWBERYS CARPETS
THE PICK OF THE WORLDS MARKETS
DURDHAM DOWNS EASTVILLE
ASPRO
SHORT
CIRCUITS
STOP
IF REQU

14. A very rare night photograph. Car 131 stands outside the Empire Theatre in Old Market. She was rebuilt from the 125 - 139 low height series. (A.B.Bishop)

15. Car 21 waits in Broadmead at a request stop to turn into Lower Union Street, sometime early in 1938. Newbery's advertisements were in blue. The tram stop was green (to match the lamp standard owned by the Corporation) with white lettering.
(J.B. Appleby Coll.)

16. Car 35 is photographed during 1915 crossing from the Horsefair junction into Lower Maudlin Street. This is a good view of the Milnes body / Peckham truck combination which really was the backbone of the fleet. Note the curtains, the wonderful hats and the sticker on the window saying WANTED ANOTHER 100,000 MEN FOR LORD KITCHENER'S ARMY - FOR KING AND COUNTRY. (Author's Coll.)

17. Further up Lower Maudlin Street comes car 35 again, but this time in the early 1930s. She is passing the spot which is now the Eye Hospital. Going through the Horsefair junction is Greyhound double decker Bristol HY3630. (Newham Library Service)

18. Saturday, 7th May 1938. This is the final day for trams on route 3 with car 107 at the Whiteladies Gate stop, collecting her last passengers for the City on a sad, wet day. She was broken up and burnt by 24th June with 33 other victims at the back of Kingswood Depot. (S.Miles Davey)

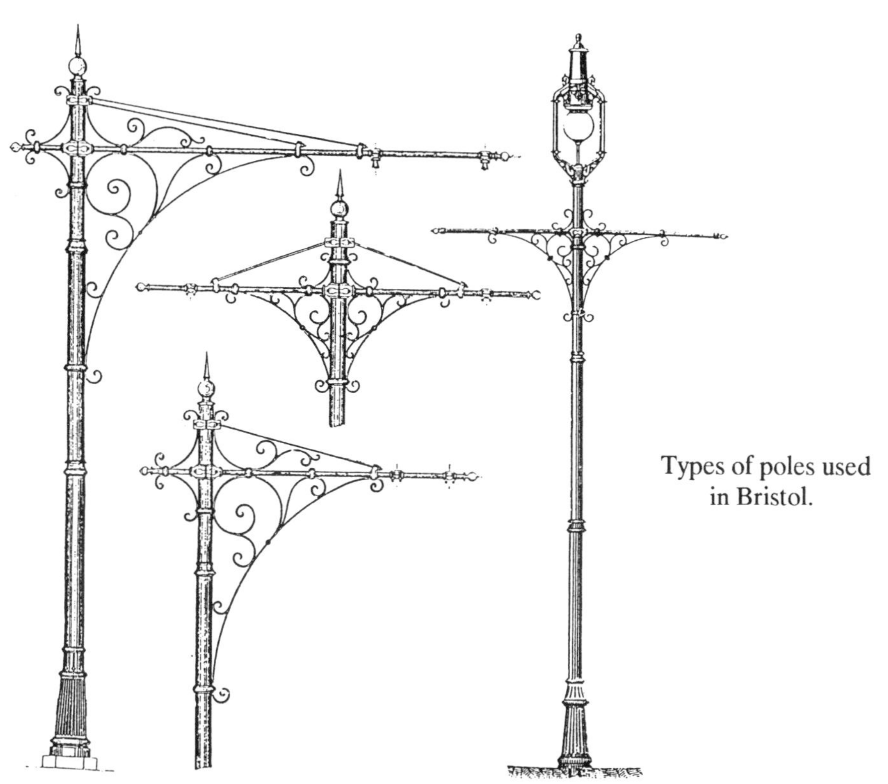

Types of poles used in Bristol.

19. Tuesday, 10th May 1938. Three days later and the tram poles are almost down. Bristol Tramways 2 ton tower wagon HT 9747 is assisting with the dismantling of the overhead. Standing by is the Tramway's Morris Commercial HW 733. A Brislington built K type replacement bus timidly ascends the hill to Durdham Downs, free from the wires that used to stretch overhead. (S.Miles Davey)

20. Car 35 again, in 1938 at the Durdham Downs terminus. Together with pictures 16 and 17, one can see how the company kept its trams permanently on the same routes. These three shots show the slight modernisation changes that were made to the original Milnes bodies, and the two styles of fleet number. (W.A.Camwell)

Tramways Centre - Durdham Downs

21. Fashions and sunshine come together to make an attractive view of three types of car at the Tramways Centre terminus. Car 37, built by Milnes, is about to leave through Magpie Park for Zetland Road and the Downs. To the left is car 145, low height with single door, built by the American Car Co; to the right is car 210, with a Bristol Wagon Co. body, built at Lawrence Hill which shows clearly the 90 degree staircase. This picture is dated 3rd February 1915. (Author's Coll.)

22. Car 119 is "fighting the tide" in Cheltenham Road, having just come under the Arches that took the GWR and Midland Railway from Montpelier to Redland. This was the famous flood of 1st July 1914. (M.J.Tozer Coll.)

23. At Zetland Road junction, car 127 waits to turn into Cheltenham Road. All the later Ovaltine advertisements were printed on paper as opposed to the usual heavy enamelled sheets. (S.Miles Davey)

24. Car 44 proudly stands at the "up" stop, which shows fare stage, whilst waiting for her driver to come out from behind the stairs. She had just been repainted and appears spotless, advertising JONES, BRISTOL'S MODERN STORE. (S.Miles Davey)

25. Having passed Redland Station, the route climbed up Redland Road. After the withdrawal, the track was soon taken up and three stages of this process are seen within a few yards. Note the various red flags. Further up on the left is the Clyde Road terminus of bus route 20. (S.Miles Davey)

26. Further up Redland Hill, we observe car 40 during the period 1917-20 as there is a conductress on the platform. Timothy West and his family lived in the middle house on the right and our family next but one. We spent many an hour watching trams from those rear windows. (Bygone Bristol)

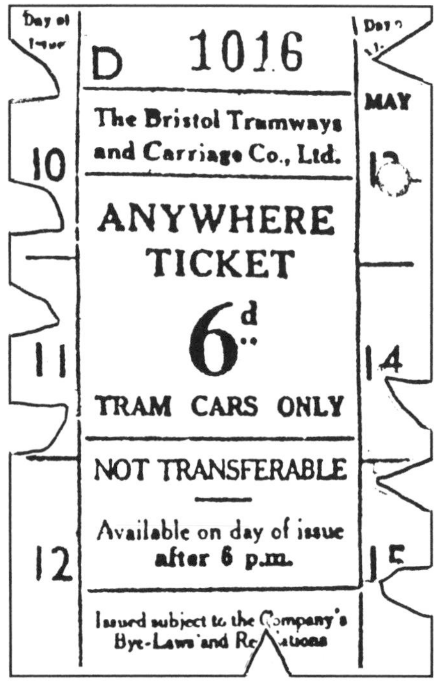

Day of Issue | D 1016 | Day of Issue

The Bristol Tramways and Carriage Co., Ltd.

ANYWHERE TICKET

6d

TRAM CARS ONLY

NOT TRANSFERABLE

Available on day of issue after 6 p.m.

Issued subject to the Company's Bye-Laws and Re[illegible]ations

10 11 12 | MAY 13 14 15

27. Almost at the terminus, crossing Stoke Road is car 203, of the 203-232 series, a stranger in the area. After rebuilding, she is seen here on a Brill 21E truck being driven by a smiling Mr.Bill Long who played cricket for the Tramways teams. (S.Miles Davey)

28. At the terminus, car 31 acts as a "stage set" for a posed crew together with the author and his sister Melody Davey. The driver, Mr. Walter Bishop was based at Horfield Depot for many years. This was taken on the last day of this route, 15th July 1939 when my father took us on the whole two-way journey. The conductor still remains unidentified. (S.Miles Davey)

REGENT
SUPER
BRITISH AND BEST
REGENT
SUPER
ELECTRIC CARS
STOP HERE
31

Tramways Centre - Ashley Down Road

29. The second car to be numbered 86 waits at the terminus on 4th September 1932. She was new in 1920 and can be seen riding on the experimental Peckham P22 truck which had a 7 ft. wheelbase. She was only used during rush hours due to the noise she made straining herself on the curves. The Bristol Company realised that the 6ft.6ins./1981mm standard wheelbase proved to be the most suitable length. (G.N.Southerden)

30. Having negotiated the St James' Barton junction (left from Centre, right from Old Market), car 49 is about to pass the Full Moon Hotel. This was, then, the main A38 road and a road sign says GLOUCESTER 34. An employee, known as a points boy, is busy with a watering can. Barton Motors have entrusted the family firm to let part of the building. (Author's Coll.)

31. Further up Cheltenham Road, car 31 returns to the city with Mr.Cyril Thomas firmly at the controls, with his conductor "up top". Car 152 is on a short working to Filton Park. Both advertise Whitbreads, having black letters on a yellow background. The Hillman on the right, ABO 784, actually belonged to a Mr. A. Bone. (S.Miles Davey)

32. About to go under the Cheltenham Road arches is car 61 on an even shorter working to Horfield Barracks. (S.Miles Davey)

33. Before laying these great junctions, they had to be tried out elsewhere. This is Zetland Road junction in such a situation but the location is unknown. Suggestions are that it may be in the Brislington area. (M.J.Tozer Coll.)

Zetland Road Junction.

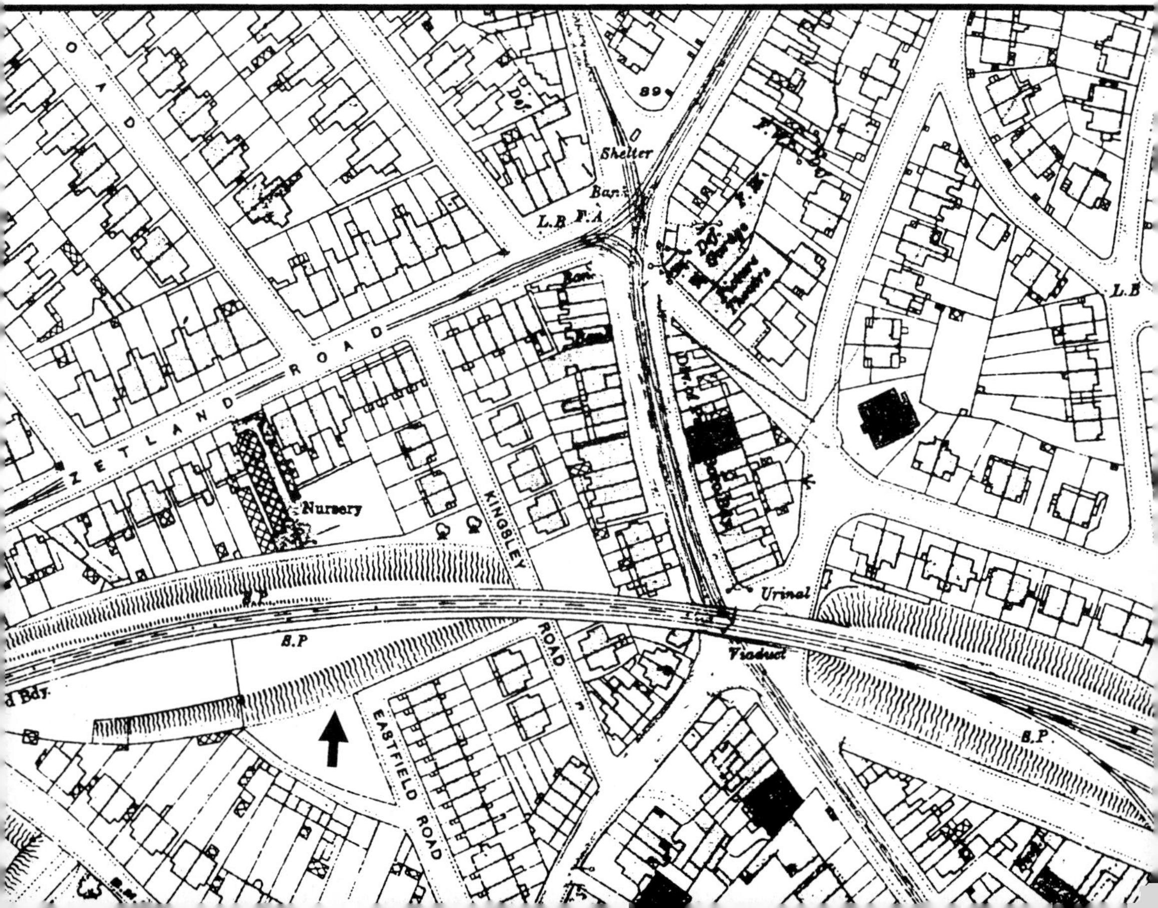

34. The junction is now in its correct place. Cheltenham Road arches are in the distance; A 28 bus to Avonmouth is about to climb Cranbrook Road. This vehicle is a Bristol G-type of the series built 1936/7 at Brislington. (H.B.Priestley)

35. Car 66 is picking up passengers further up Gloucester Road outside Beacon Motors. The Farley's advertisement displayed white letters on a black background. The Henly's paper ones were yellow. (H.B.Priestley)

WYLD'S WINES
TRAMWAYS CENTRE
HARRIS
FILTON PARK
HARRIS
58
53
34

36. The Ashley Down Road Depot could accommodate 56 trams and was sometimes known as Horfield. Cars 58, 53, 34, would use the west gate and 167, 144 and 124 would use the east, as the Victoria public house was in between the two. Interestingly, the 5 destinations are all displayed. Note the ropes hanging loose for the conductors to nurse the trolleys over the points. Originally the terminus was outside the depot before the extension to the Barracks. Some of the tracks are still down having been included as a feature outside a new health clinic. (W.A.Camwell)

Horfield Barracks - Filton

37. Up the slope from the depot was the terminus at the Barracks. Car 11 is just pulling away from the stop with the orange advertisement for Avon Tyres. (Author's Coll.)

38. The next terminus was Filton Park where Car 7 stands showing off her experimental P35 truck. When war came, this was replaced (see picture 78). The famous Bristol Brewery's advertisement showed white lettering on a bright red background. One car each day worked this shortened version of route 6. (S.Miles Davey)

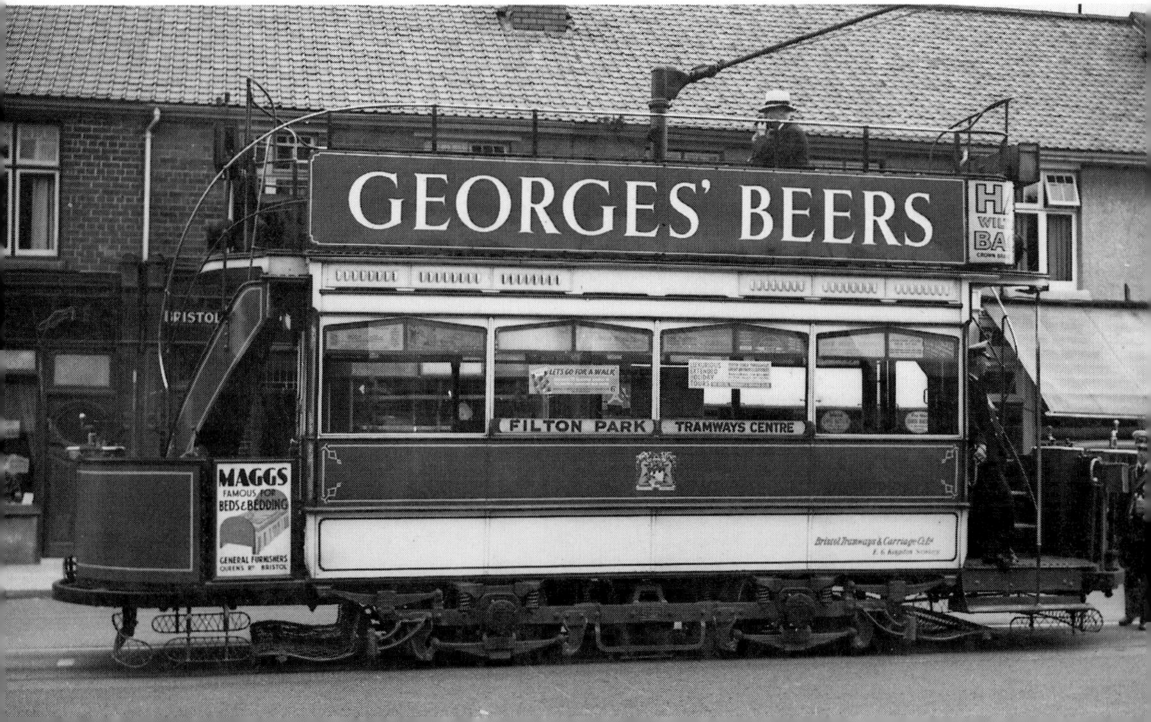

39. The final terminus at Filton was outside the entrance of the Bristol Aeroplane Company's offices. Car 55 is about to depart, and the trolley arm will use the reverser. Twice a year Jones', BRISTOL'S MODERN STORE changed to GREAT SALE. (W.A.Camwell)

Tramways Centre - Fishponds

40. Waiting on the north side of the Triangle, on the outer track, are two trams on the Fishponds route. Car 157 has an American Car Co. body on a Brill 21E truck, part of the 142 - 161 lowheight series. Behind her is 87, a 3 window, 1895 car. She was one of the original 86-97 series but now with some modernisation. The Company's offices are opposite on the right. (Author's Coll.)

41. Having left the terminus, car 155 is caught in Rupert Street. A fine example of an American Car Co. low height body. These cars were lower in order to get beneath the Midland Railway Bridge in Stapleton Road, by Eastville Park (see picture 45). The tops of the windows were curved on this series, and they had very thick ventilators. (M.J.Tozer Coll.)

42. Car 152 is at the Horsefair junction stop. She has been rebuilt from the style of car 155 (picture 41) and has a new body built at Brislington by the Tramways Company as part of the standardisation programme.
(S.Miles Davey)

43. Outgoing cars turned right and used Cumberland Street, through which the trams ran on either track. There were five crossovers in this short stretch so that parked vehicles could be passed! Coming into the city, the whole length of City Road was used (not Cumberland Street) and car 153 can here be seen coming from that direction, having just passed the Full Moon Hotel.
(Memories, Corn Exchange, Bristol)

155
EASTVILLE
HIPPODR

P.E.GANE
FURNISHING
FABRICS

44. Car 155 (see picture 41) has now been rebuilt at Brislington with a standard body. She stands at the end of Warwick Road with the Eastville Hippodrome behind. This stop was the original terminus in 1897. (H.B.Priestley)

46. Rebuilt car 142 is at Fishponds Terminus with the crew "up front" and a very young points boy is on the pavement, holding the bar for changing them. The driver has just lifted the controller handle off to take it through to the other end. All the 142-161 series were eventually standardised. (W.A.Camwell)

45. Here is car 91 (of the original 86-97 series) showing the 3 window layout. This would have been before the First World War and shows the bridge (height 16ft.2ins./4927mm) that was the reason for the low height cars to be ordered. (Author's Coll.)

Hotwells - Temple Meads Station

47. Car 223 now rebuilt, stands at the terminus at Hotwells, under the Clifton Suspension Bridge. Car 226 is on her way to the City along the lovely Avon Gorge. (W.A.Camwell)

→

48. A very early view outside the Clifton Rocks Railway of car 114 in 1900. She has a destination board, painted by hand. The Joint Station is now called Temple Meads. The Peckham wheelbase is only 6ft./1828mm with leaf springs placed inside. These were lengthened to 6ft.6ins./1981mm in the 1920s with these springs moved to the ends. The two crew are in the Victorian style of uniform. Samuel White, Managing Director - is in black letters on the rocker panel. The tram is more than likely on her first trip, exactly as new. (M.J.Tozer Collection)

49. The Clifton Rocks Railway was bought by the Bristol Tramways in 1912 and soon after the front was rebuilt as shown here. The system closed in 1934. Car 221 is passing the facade of the station with two of the staff at the entrance. Four cars worked in two pairs inside. (Author's Coll.)

BORWICKS
318

50. Routes 8 & 9 used the south side of the triangle at the Tramways Centre. Car 218 stands at the stop and for a short while she had her destination boxes raised twice as high so that advertisements could be seen when placed on the inner sides. No other car had this treatment and the idea was abandoned. This view is an enlargement of one of a set taken every 10 minutes throughout one Tuesday in March 1922.
(Bristol Tramways & Carriage Co.)

51. On the right is the elaborate Victoria Tram Sttation, which housed the ticket office. It is adjacent to Temple Meads railway station and was earlier used as stables for 208 tramway horses. Car 226 is passing the white-painted post during World War I. This is the main line to Brislington and was the terminal point for route 8. Note the beautiful ironwork to carry just two wires. (Author's Coll.)

52. This rare view of a tram in the tram station was taken in May 1925. Route 17 used this terminus to collect passengers from South Wales off the GWR and carried them to Hotwells to link with the Campbell's steamers back across the channel. Car 204 is about to leave on the short route to the Tramways Centre. When the tram station closed, Route 8 ceased and was absorbed into route 9 for Brislington. (G.N.Southerden)

53. The remaining tracks, photographed in the 1950s, amazingly are still there today. Maybe they could just be used again when Bristol gets its metro! (S.Miles Davey)

Temple Meads Station - Brislington.

54. On leaving the station, we pass Arno's Vale Cemetery and from our platform we see car 105 coming up behind us at the same moment that car 110 travels back to the Tramways Centre. The reason that there was always an odd number of seats on a top deck is clearly seen as the trolley mast always took the place of a seat so as not to be in the gangway. (Memories, Corn Exchange, Bristol)

55. The next stop is outside the famous Brislington Depot. The tramcar has just been delivered from Milnes. The decency boards are flat out along the top with the end rectangles yet to be turned 90 degrees for positioning. They were dispatched in this manner to get under the railway bridges. This early 1900/01 shot shows also one of the Midland built cars having just been assembled. The first delivery of this 1900 order arrived on 14th April. (M.J.Tozer Coll.)

56. At about the same time, preparations are evident with painters, transfer fitters and engineers working hard inside the assembly shops. Milnes arrivals are represented by cars 162 (with no lamp), 26,167 and 43. Interestingly car 125, an 1897 low height car is also there, presumably being repainted. Their destination boards have not yet been fitted. (M.J.Tozer Coll.)

57. Outside the regular running shed for the Hotwells 9s and the Knowle 10s are parked cars 217, 81, 82, 222 and 199. On the left is the Engineering Shop and even today the tracks are still visible. (S.Miles Davey)

58. From the other end looking back to the entrance are seen cars 199, 222, 82, 81, 217 and 207. Car 199 was one of the four track clearing vehicles (see picture 72). Note the additional wire on the right which makes a pair. This was placed there in order that tests could be carried out with the two trolleybuses that the Company built. (S.Miles Davey)

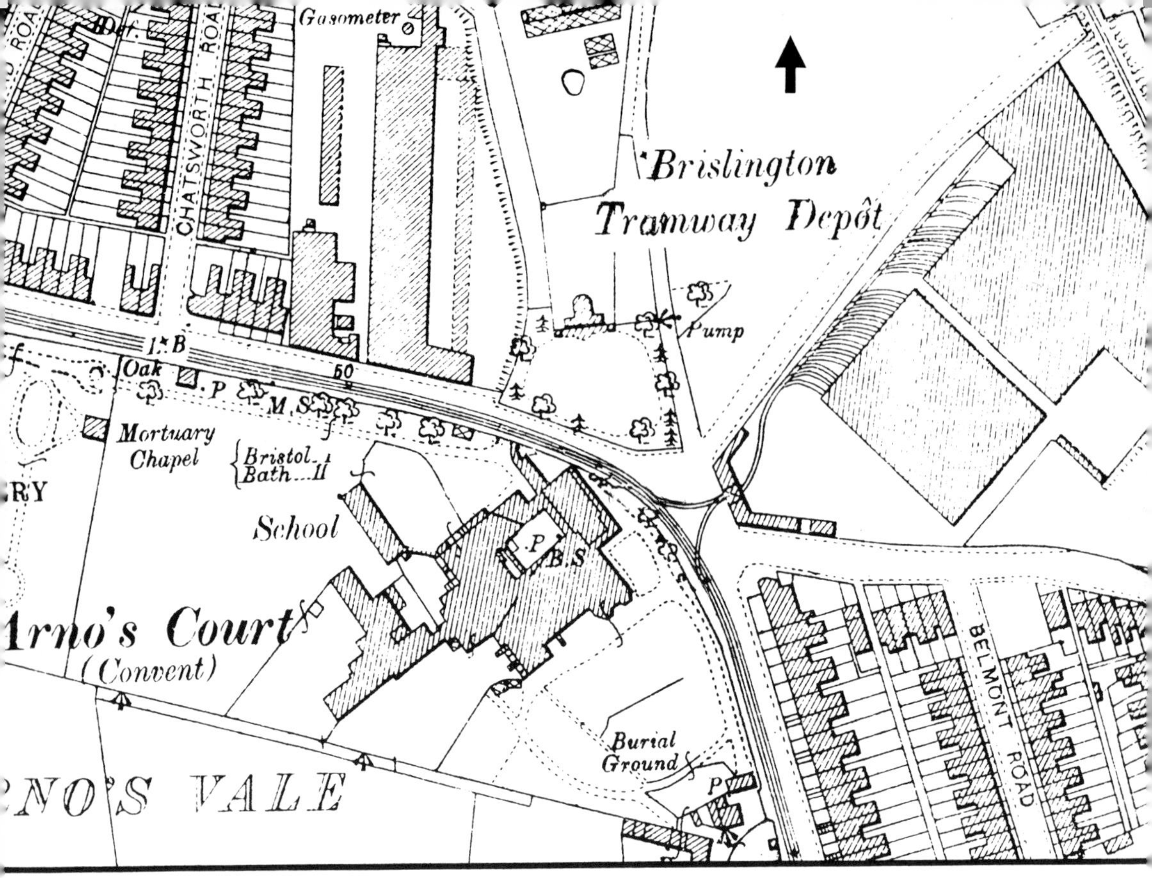

59. At Brislington terminus stands car 144 now in her rebuilt form. The destination board would have been blue letters on a yellow background. (S.Miles Davey)

Bristol Bridge - Knowle

60. Waiting outside St. Nicholas' Church, on the north side of Bristol Bridge stands car 210 showing a different body and different truck from when she was new. The driver pulls her away from the old "fruit and veg" market on the left. (H.B.Priestley)

61. Up the Wells Road, at the top of the hill, outside the George Inn, car 21 takes on passengers. She has no advertisement on the decency board which would have been painted in a dark green. (S.Miles Davey)

62. Approaching the Red Lion Inn, at the Knowle terminus, is car 73 with a driver known only as Fred who has already changed the blind ready for a return trip. Car 201 is passing on the 15 route to that lovely destination, namely, Nags Head Hill (top). She still carries the early style of fleet number whereas car 73 has the more modern figures. (S.Miles Davey)

Bristol Bridge - Ashton Road

63. Routes 11 & 12 started from the south side of Bristol Bridge, in the middle of Redcliffe Street outside E.S. & A. Robinson's offices. Car 226 is destined for Ashton Road and car 9 shows Bedminster Down. (W.A. Camwell)

64. The two routes travelled together along Redcliffe Street where car 125 waits for car 30 to clear the single track section. Note the signal discs on the post on the right that display to the driver exactly how many trams are on that stretch of track coming from the other direction. A similar signal is illustrated in companion Middleton Press volume *Kingston and Wimbledon Tramways.* The tramways of Bristol and the London United company both show the common influence of Sir James Clifton Robinson. (H.B.Priestley)

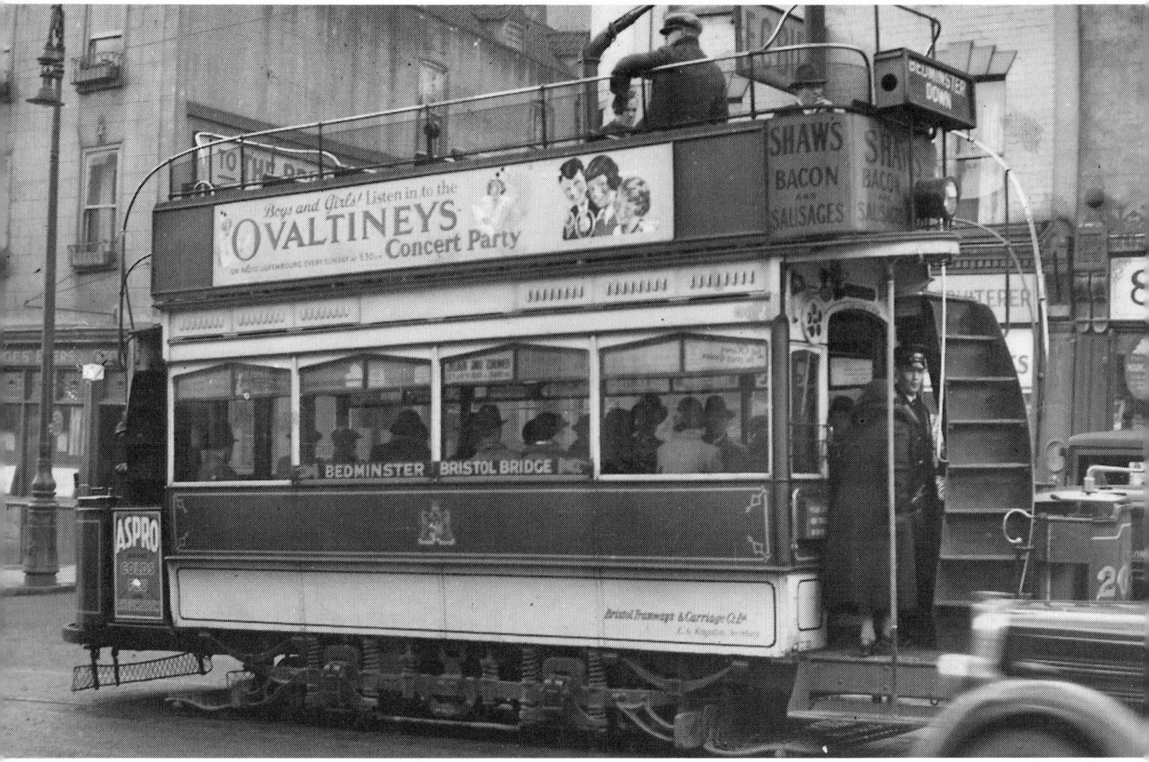
BEDMINSTER DOWN
SHAWS BACON AND SAUSAGES
Boys and Girls! Listen in to the
OVALTINEYS
Concert Party
BEDMINSTER
BRISTOL BRIDGE
ASPRO
Bristol Tramways & Carriage Co. Ltd

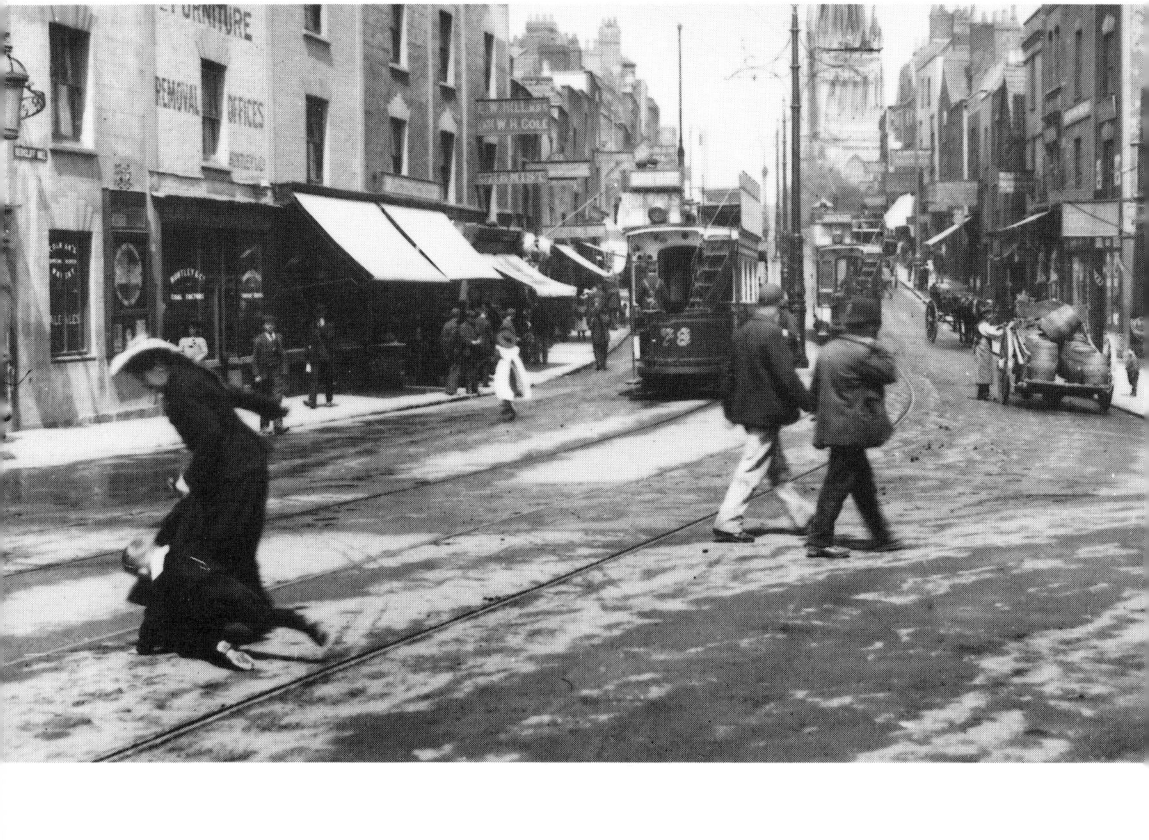
FURNITURE
REMOVAL OFFICES
W. H. COLE
78

65. Before going down Redcliffe Hill to Bedminster Bridge car 203 allows a clear view of her Brill 21E truck. Guinea Lane goes off behind to the General Hospital.
(S.Miles Davey)

66. "Get up and behave yourself". At the bottom of Redcliffe Hill around 1905 some poor little lad is having a rough ride; a tram in the 80 series approaches for Ashton whilst car 78 returns to the city. The beautiful church of St.Mary Redcliffe stands in the distance.
(Author's Coll.)

67. The two routes split at the London Inn and turning right along North Street car 71 has to negotiate the important work of a maintenance gang with a red flag and replacement blocks.
(H.B.Priestley)

68. Car 128 stands at the terminus ready to return. She shows off the EMB Company's hornless type truck which was on permanent loan to the Bristol Tramways. They even opened an office in Bristol hoping to sell more trucks, but to no avail. The two crew are seen smiling before trundling back through Bedminster and Redcliffe Street.
(S.Miles Davey)

69. Just past the passenger stop, cars were parked on a stub outside the Bristol Motor Co. Car 226, now in war time guise (see pictures 80/81), waits in the rain with the driver in his wet gear. Car 87 waits down at the passenger pick up point. This car had an EMB pivotal type truck for two years. It was so unsuitable that she never moved out of Brislington Depot for all of that time. (S.Miles Davey)

Bedminster Depot - Bedminster Down

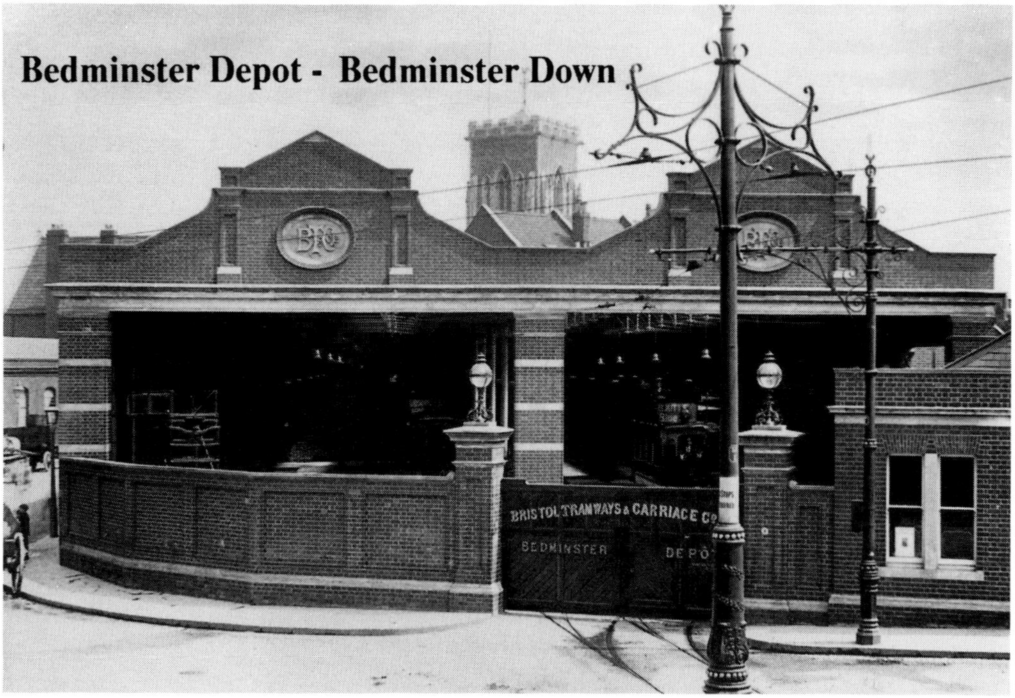

70. Between pictures 66 and 67, the Bedminster trams turned left and immediately passed the entrance to the depot, which served just the two routes, accommodating 23 cars. This is a very early 1900 view and shows, from left to right, a tower wagon which would have been horse drawn, car 107 and more than likely car 99 over the gates. The BTCCL letters can be seen in the two apexes in the roof with St. John's Church behind. (M.J.Tozer Coll.)

71. A direct hit on the morning of 4th January 1941 sadly killed a driver who had just reported for duty at 6.0am to take out a workmen's car. Trams written off around the crater included cars 236, 87, 136, 166, 71 on to which the roof has fallen and 164. The four worst victims were broken up here, but the rest were towed over to Kingswood for burning. (Author's Coll.)

72. Car 125 stands at the terminus, even though Bedminster Down was not actually reached by the trams! She has been painted to suit the blackout requirements (see pictures 80/81) and was also during the war Bedminster's track clearing car, as can be seen by the two added pieces to the ends of the truck. These pointed straight down and were useful in clearing shrapnel from the tracks. Each morning two scrapers would be attached to these pieces, one would enter the track and the other would scrape the rail surface. There were four trams adapted in this manner and they would be the first duty cars out each morning. The cars were 125 at Bedminster (replacing 164), 126 at Kingswood and 199 at St. George. (S.Miles Davey)

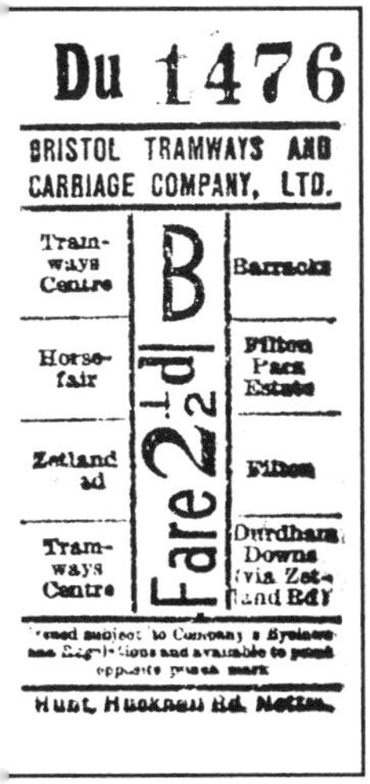

Tramways Centre - Kingswood

Du 1476

BRISTOL TRAMWAYS AND CARRIAGE COMPANY, LTD.

Tramways Centre	B	Barracks
Horsefair	Fare $2\frac{1}{2}$d	Filton Park Estate
Zetland Rd		Filton
Tramways Centre		Durdham Downs (via Zetland Rd)

Issued subject to Company's Byelaws and Regulations and available to point opposite punch mark

Hunt, Hucknall Rd, Notts.

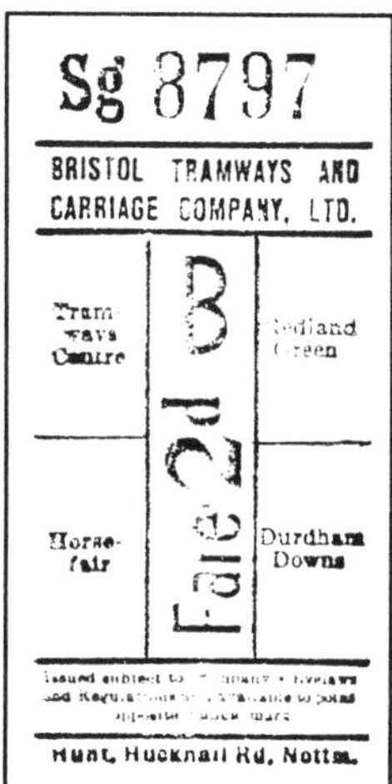

Sg 8797

BRISTOL TRAMWAYS AND CARRIAGE COMPANY, LTD.

Tramways Centre	B	Redland Green
Horsefair	Fare 2d	Durdham Downs

Issued subject to Company's Byelaws and Regulations and available to point opposite punch mark

Hunt, Hucknall Rd, Notts.

73. Here is the famous Tramways Centre. Cars 213, 23 and 67 are seen on the north side, in fact the only side now used (the buses can be seen on the Westbury and Hotwells routes). In addition to this, only one track was used; car 213's Brill 21E truck can be clearly seen. (S.Miles Davey)

74. Car 172 is on the Horsefair junction showing her 1920s style of numbering. She was the last of the Milnes delivery of 120 trams. The tracks on the left are for cars to Stokes Croft. (Newham Library Service)

Old Market area.

75. When this was taken, probably 1913, the 13 route sometimes started from here outside the Empire Theatre. Car 180 is a Midland built car whereas car 32 is a Milnes. One difference being that the bulkhead window tops on the Midland Cars have a curved line above them. She advertises HUDSONS SOAP with the three letters LNS. This means Leaves No Smell, and they were part of a Hudson promotion. Any passenger having bought soap, with these letters on the wrapper, handed in the wrapper to the conductor in return for a ticket. (Author's Coll.)

76. About to depart on 21st August 1939, car 216 uses the south tracks now that the Tramways Centre section has ceased (due to bus route 7). A Bristol K5G, registered FHT 794, has just arrived as a route 6 and will return to Filton as a 5. (H.B.Priestley)

77. Car 158, spotted climbing up through St.George in 1940, was the only one painted in the wartime livery. This was the navy blue used on the buses but without any lining. The rest of the blackout requirements have been carried out. (S.Miles Davey)

78. Further up in Two Mile Hill Road, car 7 stops at Charlton Road. She has just the basic requirements for the wartime blackout as the headlamps are still operative. The golden hands have been painted black on the destination board. Her P35 truck has now gone, replaced by a standard Peckham. (S.Miles Davey)

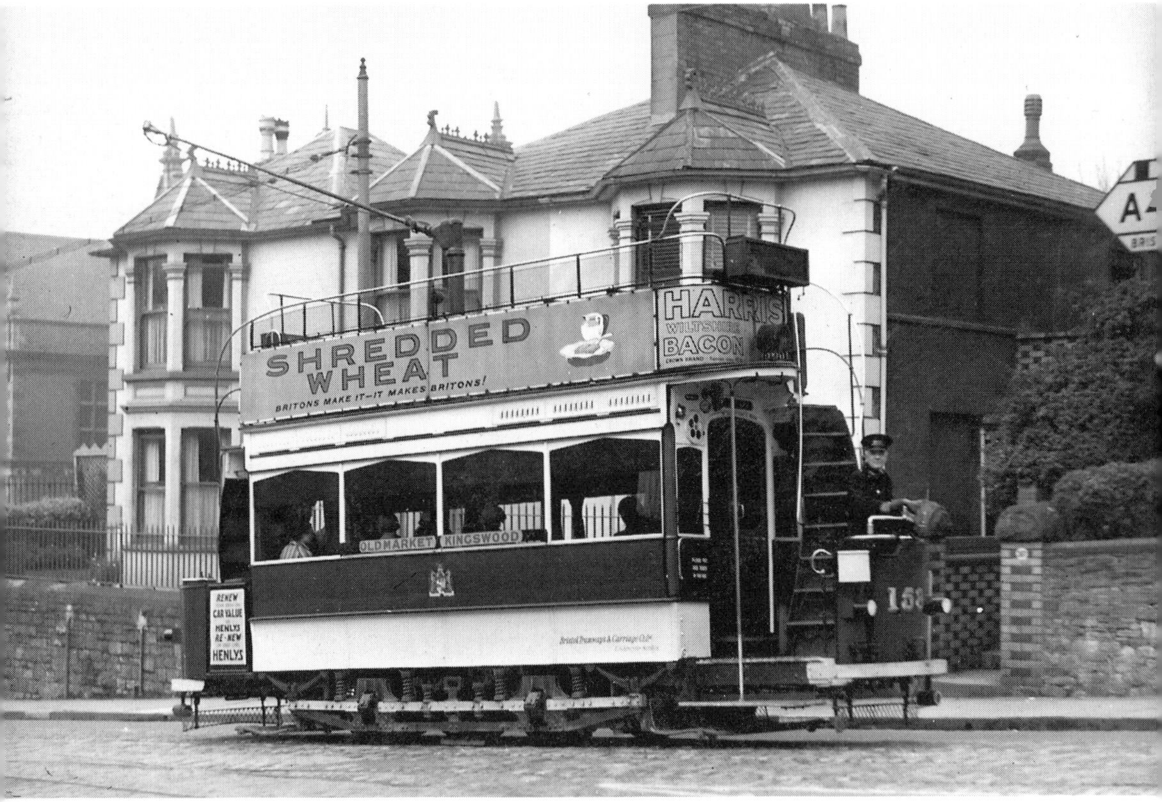

79. A few days before the opening of the electric tramways, car 41 (a converted horse trailer) is on a trial run behind one of the 86 - 97 batch. The one in front is car 88. This shows clearly how the trolley standard was well to the side. The trailer has no decency boards, therefore ladies would only travel inside! The use of trailer cars ceased on 15th January 1899. (M.J.Tozer Coll.)

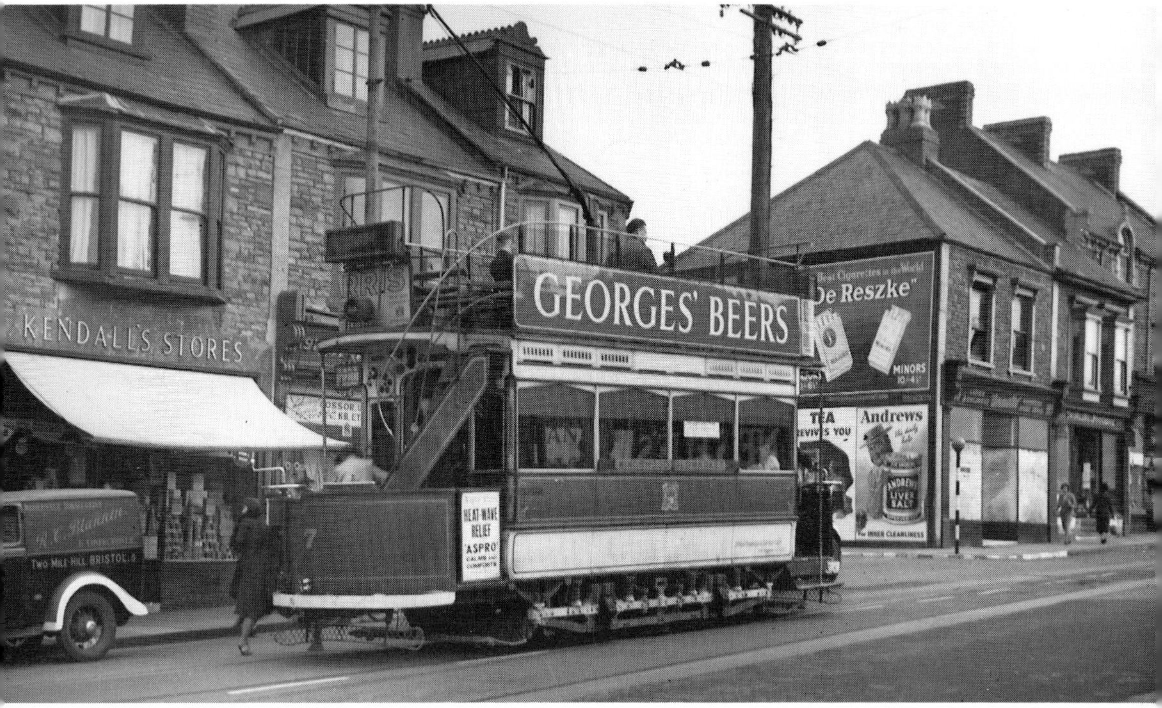
KENDALL'S STORES
GEORGES' BEERS
HEAT-WAVE RELIEF
'ASPRO'
CALMS AND COMFORTS
"De Reszke"
MINORS
TEA REVIVES YOU
Andrews
ANDREWS LIVER SALT
FOR INNER CLEANLINESS
TWO-MILE-HILL, BRISTOL. 5

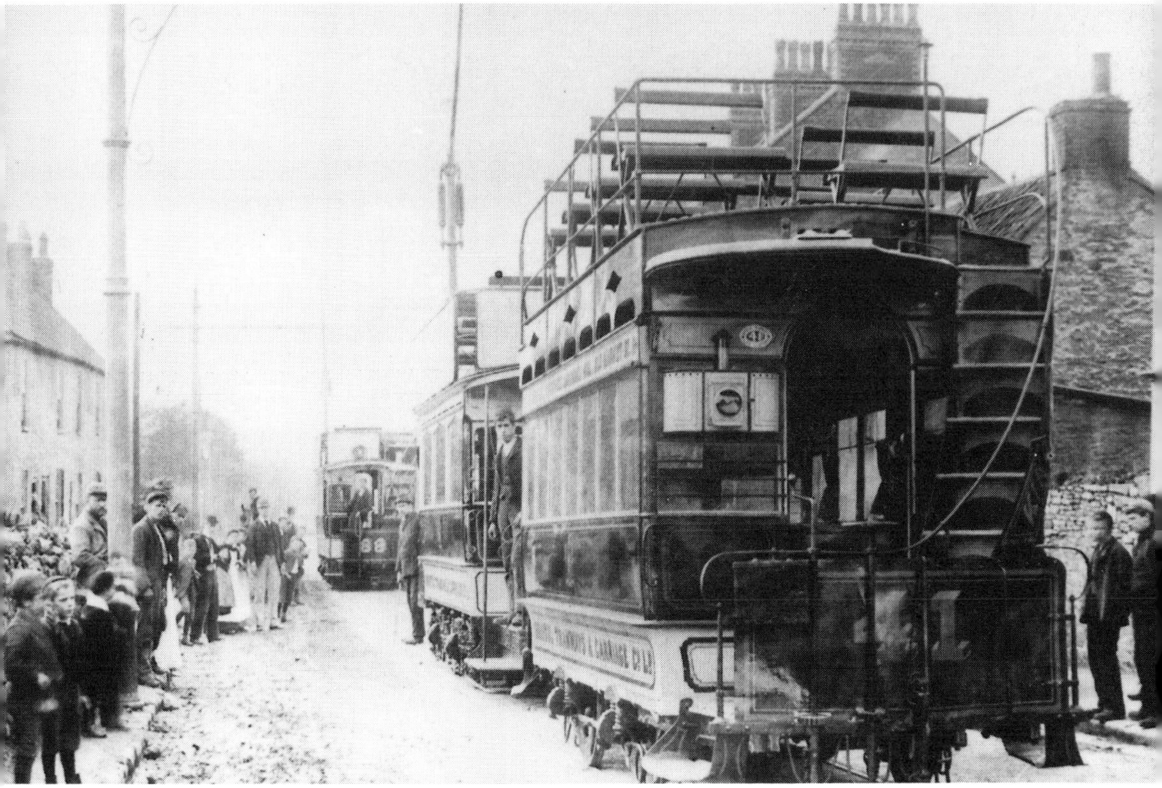
41

80. At Kingswood terminus in 1940 are two cars in slightly different war time treatments. Car 200 has had all the wartime requirements carried out, with the destination boxes, side window tops and bulkhead windows all blacked out, while the truck, platform steps, sandboxes and fenders have been whitened. Car 175 is similarly treated, but her headlamps are still operative, whereas car 200 has two small lights placed by the number with a tiny reflector at the bottom. Car 200 lasted with her Midland body for the full 41 years. (S.Miles Davey)

81. Just past the terminus is Kingswood Depot photographed probably on a Sunday morning, whilst sheltering cars 19, 216, 124, and 173 with the R A F on board. All have the complete wartime requirements to suit the blackout regulations and they all advertise HARRIS of Calne. Every tram had a similar advertisement at one end, whilst cars 1-12 and 86 had them at both ends. (M.J.O'Connor)

Zetland Road - Staple Hill

82. Car 19 is at the terminus, which was actually in Elton Road, and it will soon enter the great Zetland Road Junction. The bus stop on the left, for service 145 to Kellaway Crescent has one of the new signs QUEUE THIS SIDE OF POST, which were first tried out on 1st June 1938. (H.B.Priestley)

83. Car 138 stops in Cheltenham Road during the last week of tram service. The new bus stop post is in position to replace the old sign which will come down with the tram stop sign. The destination board on the side is one of the last, as it is stencilled and not one with letters painted by hand. (S.Miles Davey)

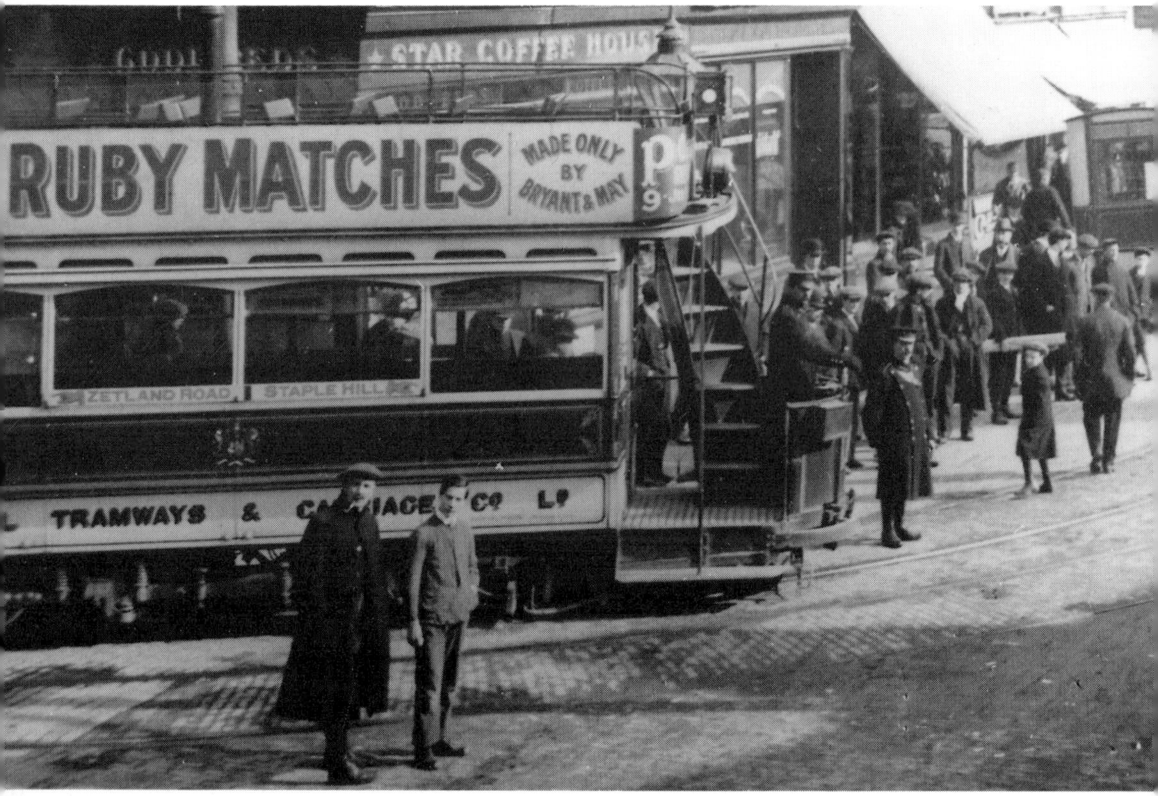

STAR COFFEE HOUSE
RUBY MATCHES
MADE ONLY BY BRYANT & MAY
ZETLAND ROAD
STAPLE HILL
TRAMWAYS & CARRIAGE Co Ld

GEORGE OLIVER
GEORGE OLIVER
OLD MARKET STREET
ZETLAND RD
SPECIALLY MADE FOR SMOKERS
SWAN VESTAS
BRITISH MADE BY BRYANT & MAY
STAPLE HILL
BRISTOL TRAMWAYS & CARRIAGE Co Ld

84. A 1914 shot of a low height car, of the 142-161 series, entering Old Market from Lower Castle Street. Note the curved tops to the windows and the thick ventilators. When this route opened the low height cars were essential for the Stapleton Road bridge. (Author's Coll.)

85. Car 156 was the last of the low height 142-161 series to run with her original American Car Co. body which shows the single door. She was photographed on 29th March 1932, on her way back to Zetland Road. When the war came, cars 156 and 144 exchanged trucks. (G.N. Southerden)

86. At the junction in Eastville, car 144 waits at the stop on the Robertson Road corner, with the Police Station behind. Compared with the previous view, this shows the double doors of the new bodies put on at Brislington. (H.B. Priestley)

87. Staple Hill Depot is sheltering cars 134, 144 and Snowplough 3 which are all standing over the pits. The latter was rebuilt from the original electric car 92 and was also used as a brushcar, as seen here on 14th July 1938. The depot would accommodate 42 trams and had a small works area. (W.A.Camwell)

88. The terminus was just past the depot (see behind car 196) on the cross roads! Car 191 is waiting outside the entrance with RESERVED showing and car 88 is in the distance as the next service car. This is the same date as the previous photo. (W.A.Camwell)

Knowle - Old Market

89. Car 197 is at the terminus ready for a shortened working to Nags Head Hill (top), whereas the destination board says St.George - Old Market - Knowle. Is the driver having a crafty smoke behind the stairs? A fine picture but the photographer is unknown. (Author's Coll.)

90. An unidentified tram has arrived at the bottom of Temple Meads incline and the tracks from the old Tram Station can be seen in the foreground. Victor Latty's, the well stocked Chemist/Photographers shop, is behind the tram. (C.E. Klapper)

91. A publicity shot taken in 1914 with vehicles posed for the event. Here the route leaves Victoria Street and turns into Bath Street. Coming the other way the tram swings out and travels wrong road for a few yards, as the Midland built tram bearing the BLACK & WHITE advertisement, either has done or will do. On the right, under the lamp, stands an employee with the stop/go board showing the white side, with a black circle. (Bristol Tramways & Carriage Co.)

TRAM CAR SERVICES

Service	Route	Weekdays First dep. A.M.	Weekdays Last dep. P.M.	Sundays First dep. P.M.	Sundays Last dep. P.M.
Service No. 11	**Bristol Bridge and Ashton Road**				
	From Ashton Road	5 25	1115	2 10	1025
	,, Bristol Bridge	5 30	1130	2 10	1030
Service No. 12	**Bristol Bridge & Bedminster Down**				
	From Bedminster Down	5 10	1120	2 15	1015
	,, From Bristol Bridge	5 30	1135	2 10	1030
Service No. 13	**T. Centre & Kingswood**				
	From Kingswood to T. Centre	5 25	1035	2 0	9 50
	,, T. Centre to Kingswood	6 5	1115	2 35	1025
	,, St. George to Kingswood	5 55	1130	2 0	1040
Service No. 14	**Zetland Road & Staple Hill**				
	From Staple Hill to Old Market	5 0	1050	1 55	9 55
	,, Fishponds to Old Market	5 5	1055	2 5	10 0
	,, Staple Hill to Zetland Road	5 10	1030	2 0	9 30
	,, Old Market to Staple Hill	5 30	1125	2 30	1025
	,, Warwick Road to Staple Hill	5 40	1130	2 0	1035
	,, Zetland Road to Staple Hill	5 55	1110	2 15	1015
Service No. 15	**Hanham, Old Market & Knowle**				
	From St. George Depot to Old Mkt.	5 4	1115	2 0	1020
	,, Hanham to Knowle	5 40	1040	2 15	9 40
	,, Old Market to St. George	5 30	1130	2 15	1035
	,, Old Market to Hanham	5 30	1120	2 15	1020
	,, Old Market to Knowle	5 40	11 5	2 15	10 5
	,, Old Market to Nags Head Hill	5 30	1120	2 15	1020
	,, Knowle to Old Market St.	5 40	1125	2 35	1025
	,, Knowle to Hanham	6 20	1055	2 35	10 0
	,, Knowle to Nags Head Hill	6 20	1055	2 35	10 0
	,, Knowle to St. George	6 20	1125	2 35	1025

Se2042

BRISTOL TRAMWAYS AND CARRIAGE COMPANY, LTD.

	B	
Eastville		Trinity Road
Warwick Road		Old Market St.
Old Market St.	Fare 1d	Park Street
Horse-fair		Tyndalls Park Rd.
Park Street		Apsley Road
Victoria Rooms		Durdh'm Downs

Issued subject to Company's Byelaws and Regulations and available to point opposite punch mark

Hunt, Hucknall Rd. Nottm.

Uf 3577

BRISTOL TRAMWAYS AND CARRIAGE COMPANY, LTD.

	B	
Eastville		Old Market Street
Warick Road		Horsefair
Armoury Square		St. Mich Hi..
Old Market Street	Fare 1½d	Tyndalls Park Rd.
Horsefair		Apsley Road
Park Street		Durdham Downs

Issued subject to Company's Byelaws and Regulations and available to point opposite punch mark

Hunt, Hucknall Rd. Nottm.

92. Outside the Hotel Vaults, a member of staff is about to sit for a few minutes on the company supplied stool after having lent the stop/go sign against the lamp standard. This board shows the red side with white circle. It was this employee's responsibility to watch for trams coming from both directions. (Author's Coll.)

"Bristol"
COMMERCIAL VEHICLES.

Accountants Department,
Stock Exchange Buildings,
Bristol 15th.November. 1933.

E.L.Babbage,Esq.,
35,Westbury Road, BRISTOL.

TELEPHONE Nº 20001
PTE BRANCH EXCHANGE.

DR TO
THE BRISTOL TRAMWAYS & CARRIAGE COMPANY LD

CHEQUES ETC. SHOULD
COMPANY

NO RECEIPT VALID EXCEPT
ON THE COMPANY'S
SEPARATE OFFICIAL FORM.

93. The main power station is being passed, during the 1914-18 War, by car 114 on the fateful St. Philip's Bridge. It was this bridge that had a direct hit, in the Second World War, and immediately finished off the system overnight. (Author's Coll.)

BRISTOL TRAMWAYS & CARRIAGE CO., LTD.

TIME TABLE.

DRAWBRIDGE, STOKES CROFT, BISHOPSTON, HORFIELD.

(Ashley Down Road.

Week Days.

DRAWBRIDGE TO HORFIELD.

First Car 7.24½ a.m., and then every 7½ minutes (at 0.2, 9½, 17, 24½, 32, 39½, 47, and 54½ in each hour). until 8.2 p.m.

After 8.2 p.m., Cars leave at 0.2, 10, 19, 27, 36, 45, and 54, in each hour, until last Car 11.10 p.m.

ZETLAND ROAD TO HORFIELD.

First Car passes at 7.41½ a.m., and then every 7½ minutes (at 0.4, 11½, 19, 26½, 34, 41½. 49, and 56½ in each hour,) until 8.19 p.m.

After 8.19 p.m., Cars pass at 0.2, 11, 19, 27, 36, 44, and 53, in each hour, until last Car 11.27 p.m.

HORFIELD TO DRAWBRIDGE.

First Car at 8.0 a.m., and then every 7½ minutes (at 0.0, 7½, 15, 22½, 30, 37½, 45, and 52½, in each hour), until 8.37½ p.m.

After 8.37½ p.m., Cars leave at 0.3, 12, 21, 30, 38, 46, and 54 in each hour, until last Car 11.46 p.m.

ZETLAND ROAD TO DRAWBRIDGE.

First Car passes at 8.10 a.m., and then every 7½ minutes (at 0.2½, 10, 17½, 25, 32½, 40, 47½, and 55, in each hour), until 8.47½ p.m.

After 8.47½ p.m., Cars pass at 0.4, 13, 22, 31, 40, 48, and 56 in each hour, until last Car, 11.56 p.m.

Sundays.

On Sundays Cars run every 7½ MINUTES. First Car departs from the Drawbridge at 2.2 p.m., the last at 10.2 p.m. First Car departs from Horfield at 2.37½ p.m., last 10.37½ p.m. Throughout Sunday, Cars depart from the Termini, and pass Zetland Road, at the same minutes in the hour as on week days (see above), when departing every 7½ minutes.

After 9.30 p.m., some Cars run to Horsefair only.

On Saturdays extra Cars run as required.

JOINT RAILWAY STATION

Every Car running to and from the Drawbridge is met by Cars to and from the Joint Station, and passengers are carried through without delay. Time occupied—30 to 35 minutes.

SPECIAL CARS may be engaged for any day other than Saturdays and Holidays, for the conveyance of Private Parties and Schools, to and from any part of the City and Suburbs where the Company have lines. No change of Cars.

PERAMBULATORS are carried on the Cars when accompanied by passengers, the fare charged being the same as for a passenger. **PARCELS,** at owner's risk, are carried when accompanied by passengers, and a fare charged if above 28-lbs. in weight. **CHILDREN** above the age of three years, whether occupying a seat or not, are charged full fare. **DOGS** are not allowed in or upon the Cars unless they be small and carried upon the lap.

Punctuality is not guaranteed, but every endeavour will be made to ensure it.

EMPIRE
VARIETY
EMPIRE
JENNINGS
BEST OF ALL
JACOBS
119

94. At Old Market, a route 15 car would arrive in behind car 213 which is a "Rush Car" on route 16 served from Brislington Depot. Car 200 is Midland built and will return to Bushy Park only. Kingswood and Staple Hill cars 115 and 137 are on the north tracks. The queue boards state WAIT HERE FOR KINGSWOOD CARS and on the right, for St. George cars. On the extreme right, the back of a signal can be seen which the driver of car 200 will have to obey before entering the single track section. (Author's Coll.)

Old Market - Hanham

95. When the Central Hall was opened on 29th April 1924, the Tramways Company hired out trams for viewing the occasion. The Princess Royal arrived at Temple Meads and carried out the duties. The Nestle's Milk car shows 15 St Aidan's Church - Old Market - Knowle. (Graphic Photo Union, London)

ESTLÉ'S MILK
SUNLIGH
SOAP
15
ST AIDANS CHURCH
OLD MARKET
KNOWLE
Fry's
DELICIOUS
CHOCOLATES
EVERY WEEKDAY

96. Just off the route is St.George Depot in Beaconsfield Road. Note the date stone, 1876. This building also became the first power station, opened in 1895, and ceased carrying out this function on 24th January 1902. Note also the bus timetables on the boards. The date stone is now a feature incorporated in the present old peoples home built on the same spot and was opened by Sir George White, the great grandson of the Company's founder, the first Sir George White. (W.A.Camwell)

97. Having just split from the Kingswood route, car 61 leaves St. George Fountain in her wartime guise. The stop sign on the left reads- ELECTRIC CARS TO CITY STOP HERE. (S.Miles Davey)

98. A rebuilt Midland car 192 is at Nags Head Hill (top), with the regulation wartime treatment. Curtains can clearly be seen, partly pulled. The destination board has very small stencilled letters, touched up by hand. (S.Miles Davey)

99. The Hanham terminus was outside the bus depot and car 139 waits there on 17th April 1939. The reverser for the trolley can be clearly seen, and will be used when the tram departs. (H.B.Priestley)

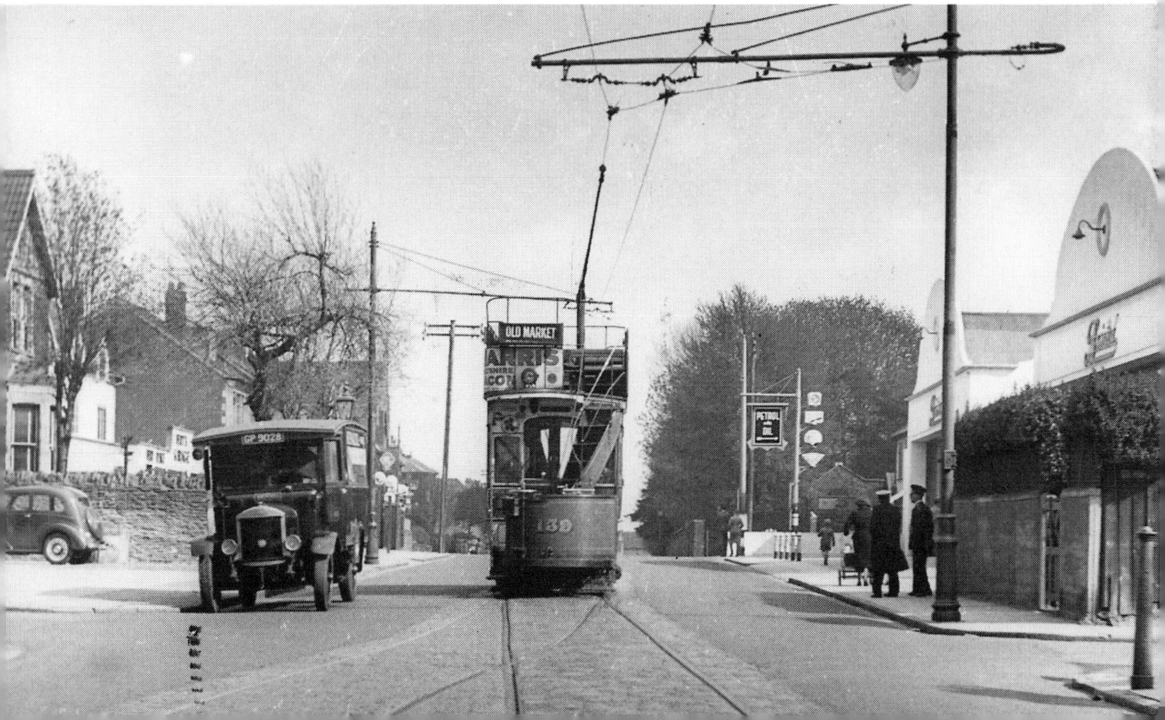

Rolling Stock

Fleet list

Abbreviations

BTCCL = Bristol Tramways & Carriage Co. Ltd.
C = Cantilever
EMB = Electro-Mechanical Brake Co. Ltd.

Gauge standard = 4ft. 8 1/2ins./1435mm

Car Nos.	Built	Builder	Seats inside/outside	Truck(s)	
1 - 6	1875	Starbuck	16/20	Horse Cars	(i)
7 - 44				Horse Cars	(ii)
45		(Single deck)	18-Later 18/16	Horse Cars	
46 - 49		(Single deck)	8 rows	Horse Cars	
50 - 70	1881		20/22	Horse Cars	
71 - 77	1883	Metropolitan	20/22	Horse Cars	
78 - 85	1892	Milnes	18/16	Horse Cars	
86 - 97	1895	Milnes	18/25	Peckham.C	(iii)
98 - 100	1895	Milnes	18/26	Horse Cars	
101 - 115	1895	Milnes	18/26	Horse Cars	(iv)
116 - 118	1896	Milnes	18/25	Peckham.C	
119 - 124	1896	Milnes	20/26	Horse Cars	
125 - 139	1897	Milnes	24/29	Peckham.C	
140	1897	Milnes	24/29	Brill 21E	
141	1897	Brill	22/25	Brill 21E	
142 - 161	1898	American Car	24/29	Brill 21E	
1 - 85	1900/1	Milnes	24/29	Peckham.C	
98 - 115	1900/1	Milnes	24/29	Peckham.C	
119 - 124	1900/1	Milnes	24/29	Peckham.C	
162 - 172	1900/1	Milnes	24/29	Peckham.C	
173 - 202	1900/1	Midland	24/29	Peckham.C	
203 - 232	1900/1	Bristol Wagon	24/29	McGuire	
86	1920	BTCCL	24/29	Peckham P22	(iii)
233 - 237	1920	BTCCL	24/29	Peckham.C	
1,2	c.1901	McGuire	Snowploughs	McGuire	
3 (ex 92)	1923	BTCCL	Snowplough	Peckham.C	
1 (ex 86)	1920	BTCCL	Rail Grinder	Peckham.C	
2 (ex 97)	1929	BTCCL	Rail Grinder	Peckham.C	

(i) - Four of these were converted for being pulled by Steam locomotives.
(ii) - Not enough information has come to light. Photographic evidence shows that some had 6 side windows and some 7. A few were converted as trail cars behind electric cars 86 - 97.
(iii) - There were two 86s, the first was rebuilt as a Rail Grinder. In 1920 a new car was built and the blank number 86 was re-allocated.
(iv) - Later converted, as trail cars behind electric cars, 86 - 97.

CARS 1-85. Horse Cars. No further information, other than that shown in the Fleet List above, has come to light. Nos 78-85 were invoiced by Milnes for £165 each. (see pictures 100/101)

CARS 86-97. "Kingswood Cars" as Charles Challenger described them. Bristol's first electric trams. 3 window bodies; 5ft.6ins./1676mm wheelbase; 15ft.9ins./4800mm high without trolley arm (see picture 102). Three more came the year after, being 116 to 118. Except for 86, 92, 97, 116 and 117, all appeared standardised with new Peckham 6ft.6ins./1981mm trucks and Brislington bodies.

CARS 98-115. Horse trailers, 3 window bodies. Except for 98-100, they were adapted for being pulled by the electric cars above (see picture 102).

CARS 119-124. Some more horse cars were still required for the Tramways Centre - Redland route, and the new extension from Totterdown to Arno's Vale. So another order for six was placed. These had 7 window bodies.

CARS 125-139. "Staple Hill Cars" as Charles Challenger described these, for the second electric route. Longer than the earlier batch, they had 4 window bodies and were also known as the low height cars, being 14ft.8ins./4470mm high without trolley arm. They were built specifically for going under the Stapleton Road railway bridge (see picture 103). Later all were standardised.

CAR 140. As above, but on a Brill 21E truck. The first to be ordered, on 29th July 1897, and delivered to any British company (see picture 104). Later she was standardised, keeping her Brill truck.

CAR 141. The J.G.Brill Company of Philadelphia shipped a demonstration tram over to the 1897 exhibition at the London Aquarium in Westminster. This was with a view to securing a contract for cars expected to be needed by the London County Council after the latter had acquired the tramways of North London in 1896. The orders were not realised and the car was sold to BTCCL and therefore was the only second hand car Bristol owned. She was numbered 141 and with some splendour was rebuilt as a directors' car, having her 22 inside seats taken out and replaced by individual bucket seats on a plush carpet and was used to inaugurate ten extensions of the tramways. She had five windows each side, no destination boxes, no advertisements, no L after BTCC which was placed twice on both sides. All metal work was plated, all paintwork was in a light blue and cream, ornately lined and panelled (see picture 106). After the opening of the extension from Durdham Downs to Westbury in 1908, she was then used as a private charter car. But, whilst going through dozens of photographs of the Tramways Centre, she was spotted in use as a passenger car in a photograph dated March 1922 (see picture 107). Finally, she was rebuilt as a standard four window car and kept her Brill 21E truck until withdrawn in 1938 and finally burnt at Kingswood in June of that year.

CARS 142-161. The second low height batch. American Car Co. bodies with trucks by Brill (see picture 108). Later all were standardised.

CARS 1-85, 98-115, 119-124, 162-172. Further cars were required and an order was placed at Milnes for 180. As they could only deliver 120 they had to contract out 60 (see below). Except for car 13 on the latest Brill 21E, all were delivered on Peckham Cantilever trucks. The first three blocks of fleet numbers were reallocated after the horse trams were scrapped or sold (see picture 109).

CARS 173 - 202. They were sub-contracted to the Midland Railway Carriage & Wagon Co. at Shrewsbury (see picture 110).

CARS 203 - 232. They were sub-contracted to the Bristol Wagon & Carriage Co. at Lawrence Hill, Bristol (no' connection with the Bristol Tramways & Carriage Co.). These cars were without doubt a disaster. The McGuire Columbian trucks were soon disposed of and the bodies were also rebuilt - probably scrapped and new ones built (see picture 111).

CAR 86. A chance to try out a different truck was offered by Peckham - their P22 which was the 7ft./2133mm version. So a new body was built by BTCCL and the 86 number, being vacant, was re-allocated (see picture 29).

CARS 233 - 237. A further 5 cars were required and these were pure Bristol Tramways. Brislington bodies were built on the standard Peckham trucks and these cars remained the same for their 20 or so years (see picture 112).

WORKS CARS 1 & 2. These served as snowploughs and brushcars. The latter survived until the end (see picture 114). No. 3 was converted from car 92 in 1923 and still ran on the early Peckham 5ft.6ins./1676mm truck (see picture 87).

WATER CAR. One is reported in Tramway & Railway World of 8th June 1905 and may have been built by the Bristol company of Brecknell, Munro & Rogers Ltd, in 1901.

RAILGRINDERS 1 & 2. They were converted from cars 86 and 97. They were, in effect, now single deckers. They had a ladder for going onto the roof for attending to trees, branches etc; they had carborundum blocks that could be forced down onto the rails; they had two water tanks inside for supplying the water to keep the blocks cool and they had canopy covers for the drivers - the only two in the whole fleet that did (see picture 115).

STEAM LOCOS 1-7. Built by Hughes Locomotive & Tramways Co. in 1880 for the route from Horsefair junction to Horfield (Egerton Road). They were kept at Whitson Street depot which is now the Badgerline Bus Station. No.2 was named "Colston" and No. 6 was named "Loughborough".

STEAM LOCO 8. Built by Fox,Walker & Co. in 1877 but loaned for the route from Old Market to Redland, Apsley Road in 1880 (see picture 100).

The motors were made by the General Electric Co. except for the 203-232 series which had the Westinghouse type.

The controllers were made by the General Electric Co. for the earlier cars up to 161. For the great 1900/01 order they were made by British Thomson-Houston, except again for the 203-232 series which received them from Westinghouse.

The system ran on 550 volts.

Fleet as in 1937

During the 1920s and 1930s, the company almost succeeded in rebuilding all its cars to the same standard design. Only a very few kept their original bodies for the full 41years. The list below gives the situation as far as can be ascertained from photographic evidence. This is not an official company list.

1-6	Peckham C	Milnes or BTCCL
7	Peckham P35	Milnes or BTCCL
8-85	Peckham C	Milnes or BTCCL
86	Peckham P22	BTCCL
87-91,93-96	Peckham C	BTCCL
98-115	Peckham C	Milnes or BTCCL
118	Peckham C	BTCCL
119-124	Peckham C	Milnes or BTCCL
125-127	Peckham C	BTCCL
128	EMB Hornless	BTCCL
129-139	Peckham C	BTCCL
140-161	Brill 21E	BTCCL (i)
162-172	Peckham C	Milnes or BTCCL
173-202	Peckham C	Midland or BTCCL
203-232	Peckham C	BTCCL (ii)
233-237	Peckham C	BTCCL

(i) Except for the following which were on Peckham C 142-144, 149, 152, 155, 158, 161.

(ii) Except for the following which were on Brill 21E 203,206,211,213,219,229.

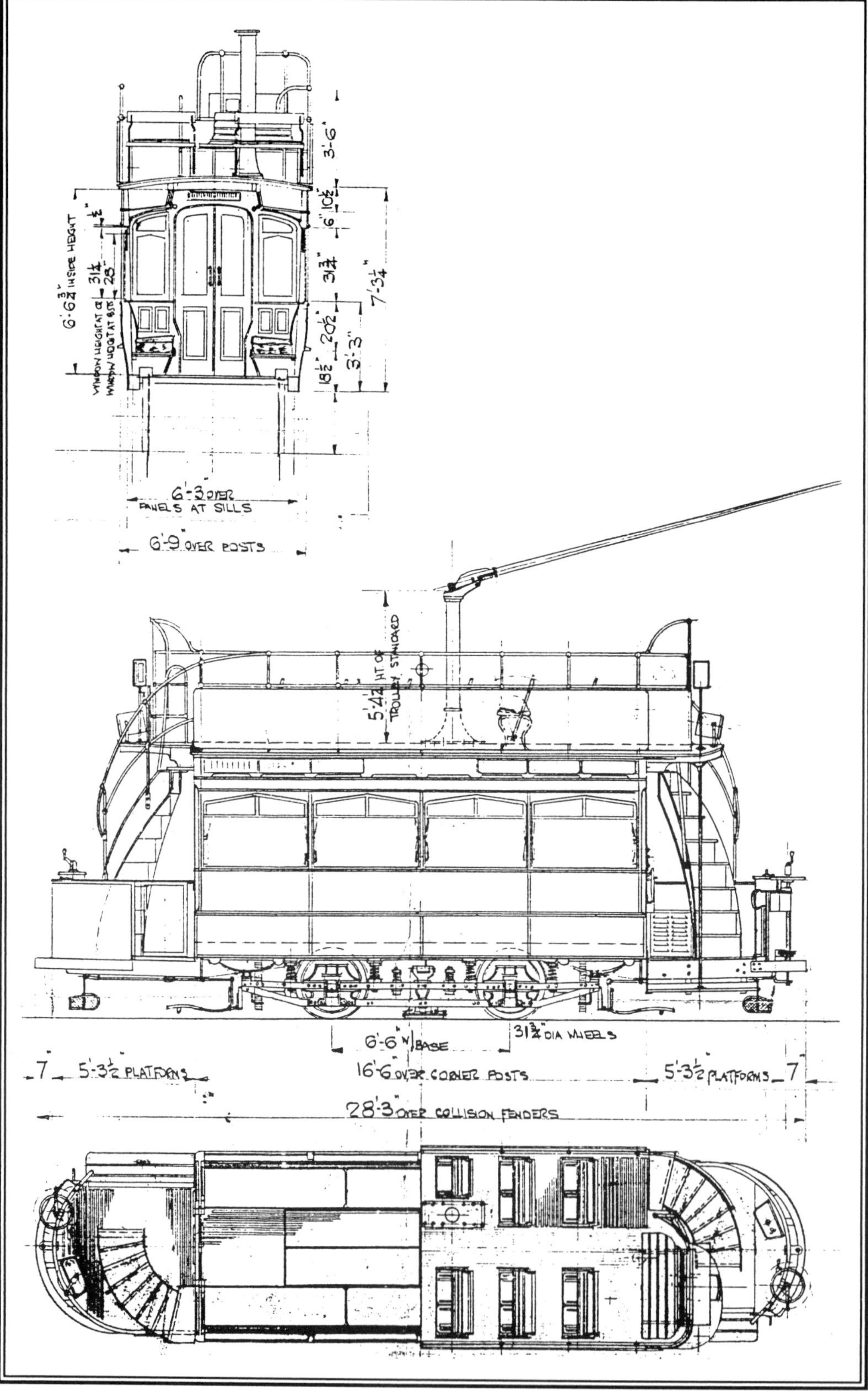

3'-6"
10¼"
6"
31¼"
7'-3¼"
20½"
3'-3"
18½"
6'-6¾" INSIDE HEIGHT
WINDOW HEIGHT AT ℄
WINDOW HEIGHT AT P.STS
31¼
28"
6'-3" OVER PANELS AT SILLS
6'-9" OVER POSTS
5'-4½" HT. OF TROLLEY STANDARD
6'-6" W/BASE
31¾" DIA WHEELS
7" 5'-3½" PLATFORMS
16'-6" OVER CORNER POSTS
5'-3½" PLATFORMS 7"
28'-3" OVER COLLISION FENDERS

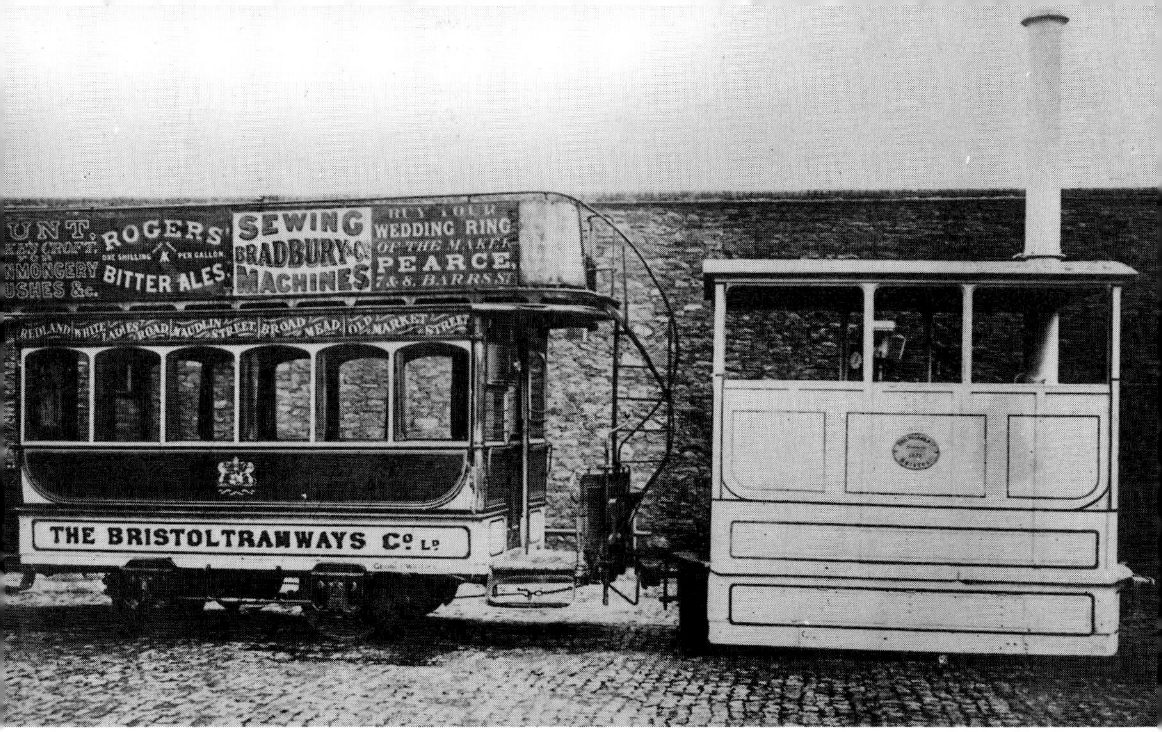

100. Series 1-6. Car 1 has been adapted for being pulled by steam locomotive No 8. (Fox, Walker & Co.)

101. An unidentified horse trailer car, one with 7 windows on the Hotwells route. SUSPENSION BRIDGE refers to the famous Clifton Suspension Bridge situated above the terminus at Hotwells. (Author's Coll.)

102. Series 86-97, 116-118. The first electric cars. This is car 90 probably just before the opening in 1895. The 98-115 trailers were the same, with three windows, but without the Peckham trucks. (Author's Coll.)

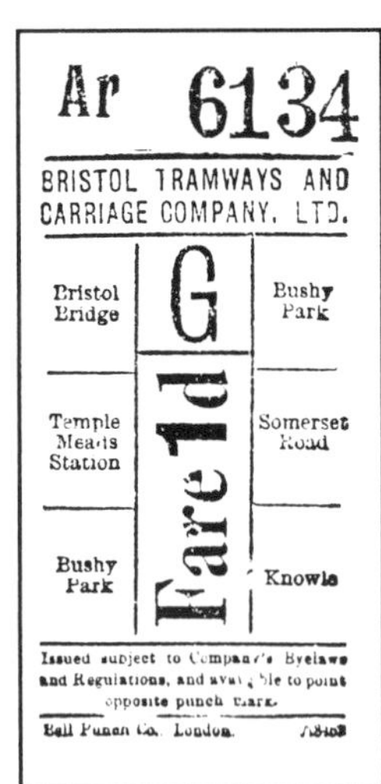

Ar 6134

BRISTOL TRAMWAYS AND CARRIAGE COMPANY, LTD.

Bristol Bridge	G	Bushy Park
Temple Meads Station	Fare 1d	Somerset Road
Bushy Park		Knowle

Issued subject to Company's Byelaws and Regulations, and available to point opposite punch mark.

Bell Punch Co. London.

103. Series 125-139. The "Staple Hill" cars, low height of 1897. Car 134 shows the longer four window Milnes body, wooden destination board and Dick Kerr trolley mast. (J.B.Appleby Coll.)

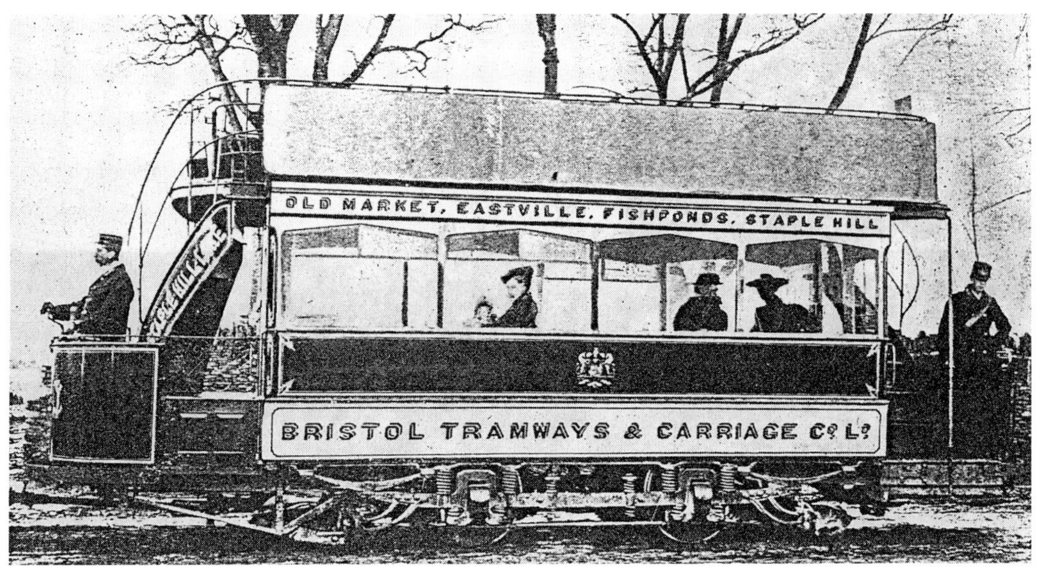

104. Car 140 is equipped with a Brill 21E truck, the first to be delivered to a British company. (J.H.Price Coll.)

Bg 5548

The Bristol Tramways and Carriage Company Limited.

ADULT

CHILD

2d.

TRANSFER SECTIONS

ADULT

CHANGE AT TRAMWAYS CENTRE

Issued subject to the Company's Bye-laws and Regulations.

105. This interior view shows the seating, floor, curtains, straps and a Pickfords advertisement, "Removals and Storage". (S.Miles Davey)

106. When first brought to Bristol, car 141 was painted in a light blue livery and is seen here at Eastville terminus. (Bristol Tramways & Carriage Co.)

107. Car 141 was later converted back for passenger use. Here she is seen at the Tramways Centre in 1922 during a 5pm rush hour, working the Fishponds route. (Author's Coll.)

108. Series 142-161. Car 161 shows the curved tops to the side windows, the single door and the thick ventilators, while at the Staple Hill terminus. (M.J.Tozer Coll.)

TRAMWAY SERVICES IN THE CITY OF BRISTOL

	Weekdays.		Sundays.	
	First dep. a.m.	Last dep. p.m.	First dep. p.m.	Last dep. p.m.
ramways Centre, Durdham Down and Westbury-on-Trym				
From Tramways Centre to Westbury	5 30	11 0	2 20	10 0
,, Tramways Centre to Durdham Down	5 30	1120	2 20	1020
,, Durdham Down to Westbury	5 30	1110	2 20	1015
,, Westbury to Tramways Centre	5 45	11 5	2 30	1010
,, Westbury to Durdham Down	5 45	1125	2 30	1030
,, Durdham Down to Tramways Centre	5 50	1115	2 20	1020
astville, Old Market and Durdham Down				
From Eastville to Old Market	5 20	1125	2 0	1030
,, Eastville to Durdham Down	5 20	1050	2 0	9 45
,, Old Market to Durdham Down	5 35	11 0	2 10	10 0
,, Old Market to Eastville	5 35	1140	2 15	1045
,, Durdham Dn. to O. Market & Eastville	6 20	1120	2 30	1020
ramways C. & Durdham D. (via Zetl'd Rd)				
From Tramways Centre to Durdham Down	6 30	1115	2 20	1015
,, Durdham Down to Tramways Centre	7 0	1115	2 30	10 5
,, Durdham Down to Zetland Road......	7 0	1140	2 30	1040
ramways Centre, Horfield and Filton				
From Ashley Down Rd. to Tramways Centre	4 50	1115	2 0	1020
,, Tramways Centre to Filton	5 20	1115	2 20	1010
,, Filton to Tramways Centre	4 40	11 5	2 10	1010
,, Filton to Ashley Down Road	4 40	1140	2 10	1040
,, Tramways Centre to Horfield Barracks	5 20	1120	2 20	1025
ramways Centre, Eastville and Fishponds				
From Fishponds to Tramways Centre	4 50	1050	2 0	9 55
,, Warwick Road to Tramways Centre...	5 0	11 0	2 0	10 5
,, Tramways Centre to Fishponds	5 20	1120	2 30	1025
otwells, Tramways Centre & Brislington				
From Brislington to Hotwells	5 25	1050	2 10	10 0
,, Brislington to Tramways Centre........	5 25	1120	2 10	1025
,, Hotwells to Tramways Centre	5 35	1125	2 30	1030
,, Tramways Centre to Brislington........	5 35	1130	2 15	1030
,, Hotwells to Brislington	5 35	1120	2 30	1020
,, Tramways Cen. to Temple Meads Stn.	5 35	1140	2 15	1045
,, Temple Meads Stn. to Tramways Cen.	5 15	1135	2 10	1040

	Weekdays.		Sundays.	
	First dep. a.m.	Last dep. p.m.	First dep. p.m.	Last dep. p.m.
Bristol Bridge and Knowle				
From Knowle	5 25	1130	2 20	1030
,, Bristol Bridge.......... .... (Bath St.)	5 45	1140	2 15	1020
Bristol Bridge and Ashton Road				
From Ashton Road..................................	5 25	1115	2 10	1030
,, Bristol Bridge	5 30	1130	2 15	1035
Bristol Bridge and Bedminster Down				
From Bedminster Down	5 10	1115	2 15	1020
,, Bristol Bridge	5 30	1130	2 10	1035
Tramways Centre and Kingswood				
From Kingswood to Old Market	5 15	1055	1 55	10 0
,, Kingswood to Tramways Centre........	5 25	1035	1 55	9 50
,, Tramways Centre to Kingswood........	6 5	1115	2 35	1025
,, St. George to Kingswood	5 55	1140	2 0	1050
,, Old Market to Kingswood	5 45	1125	2 25	1035
Zetland Road and Staple Hill				
From Staple Hill to Old Market	5 0	11 0	1 55	10 5
,, Fishponds to Old Market	5 5	11 5	2 5	1015
,, Staple Hill to Zetland Road	5 10	1030	2 0	9 30
,, Old Market to Staple Hill	5 35	1130	2 25	1035
,, Warwick Road to Staple Hill	5 40	1140	2 0	1045
,, Zetland Road to Staple Hill..............	5 55	1110	2 40	1015
Hanham, Old Market and Knowle				
From St. George Depot to Old Market	5 0	1115	2 0	1020
,, Hanham to Knowle	5 40	1040	2 15	9 40
,, Old Market to St. George	5 30	1145	2 15	1045
,, Old Market to Hanham....................	5 30	1120	2 15	1020
,, Old Market to Knowle	5 45	11 5	2 15	10 5
,, Old Market to Nags Head Hill.........	5 30	1125	2 15	1030
,, Knowle to Old Market	5 25	1125	2 35	1025
,, Knowle to Hanham	6 20	11 0	2 35	10 0
,, Knowle to Nags Head Hill	6 20	11 5	2 35	1010
,, Knowle to St. George	6 20	1125	2 35	1025

Destination blind

DURDHAM DOWNS VIA WHITELADIES ROAD
WESTBURY
EASTVILLE
OLD MARKET
DURDHAM DOWNS VIA ZETLAND ROAD
TRAMWAYS CENTRE
HORFIELD BARRACKS
ASHLEY DOWN RD
FILTON
ZETLAND RD
FISHPONDS
TEMPLE MEADS STATION
TRAMWAYS CENTRE
FILTON PARK
BRISLINGTON
BRISLINGTON DEPOT
ARNO'S VALE
HOTWELLS

BRISLINGTON DEPOT
ARNO'S VALE
HOTWELLS
TRAMWAYS CENTRE
KINGSWOOD
ASHTON ROAD
BRISTOL BRIDGE
BEDMINSTER DOWN
BEDMINSTER DEPOT
KNOWLE
HANHAM
STAPLE HILL
ZETLAND RD
NAGS HEAD HILL (TOP)
ST GEORGE
OLD MARKET
RESERVED
MARLING RD
WHITEWAY RD

109. Series 1-85, 98-115, 119-124, 162-172. Car 39 stands at Durdham Downs. It is typical of the Milnes/Peckham main delivery of 1900/1 and shows the leaf springs placed inside, wooden destination board, the route painted on the cantrail and a Victorian uniformed crew (note two horse buses behind the tram - one for Henleaze). (Author's Coll.)

THE BRISTOL TRAMWAYS

AND

CARRIAGE COMPANY, Ltd.

SPECIAL TRAMWAY CARS

BY ARRANGEMENT

110. Series 173-202. Shrewsbury-built Midland car 182 was photographed at Old Market just after World War I. The curved line above the bulkhead window and the thick/thin cantrails are the only two clues for identifying this batch of 30. (Author's Coll.)

111. Series 203-232 had Bristol Wagon & Carriage Co. bodies on McGuire Columbian trucks. Car 222 is at Hotwells and shows the 90 degree staircase. The picture also shows how these trucks seemed to bend the tram bodies down both front and back, making the base curved. Even one of the advertisements seems to be slipping away from the window top! All 30 soon reappeared from Brislington looking rather new. (Bygone Bristol)

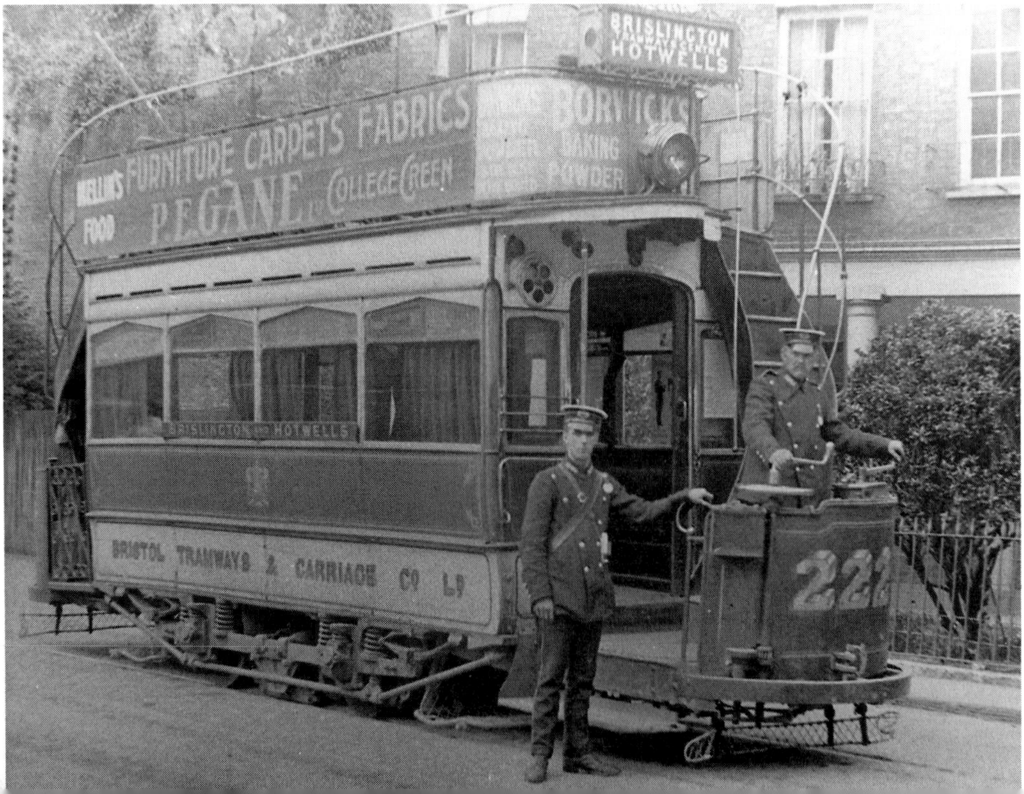

112. Series 233-237. Built 1920 by the company itself, for use from Ashley Down Road. Car 237 is at Westbury terminus with a Hudson's advertisement and the letters QAS meaning "Quick and Safe" (see picture 75). (S.Miles Davey)

113. For six Christmases from 1922 to 1927 a tram would be decorated by the employees at Brislington (in their own time) for collecting for the Lord Mayor's fund. The picture shows car 17, in 1922. The amount collected was £1171-16s-1d and used 525 bulbs! For the next three years, cars 2, 176 and 39 were used. After each Christmas new bodies would have been built for them. Car numbers for the last two years are not known. (Author's Coll.)

114. Snowplough no.2 at Brislington Depot in May 1938 is fitted out as a sweeper car. Works cars did not show their fleet numbers in their later lifetimes. (G.Baddeley)

115. Railgrinder no.2 is about to be broken up at Kingswood in 1938. Her truck was built from parts of car 97 in 1929 and was one of two such cars whose work was carried out when the tram services had ceased at night time. (S.Miles Davey)

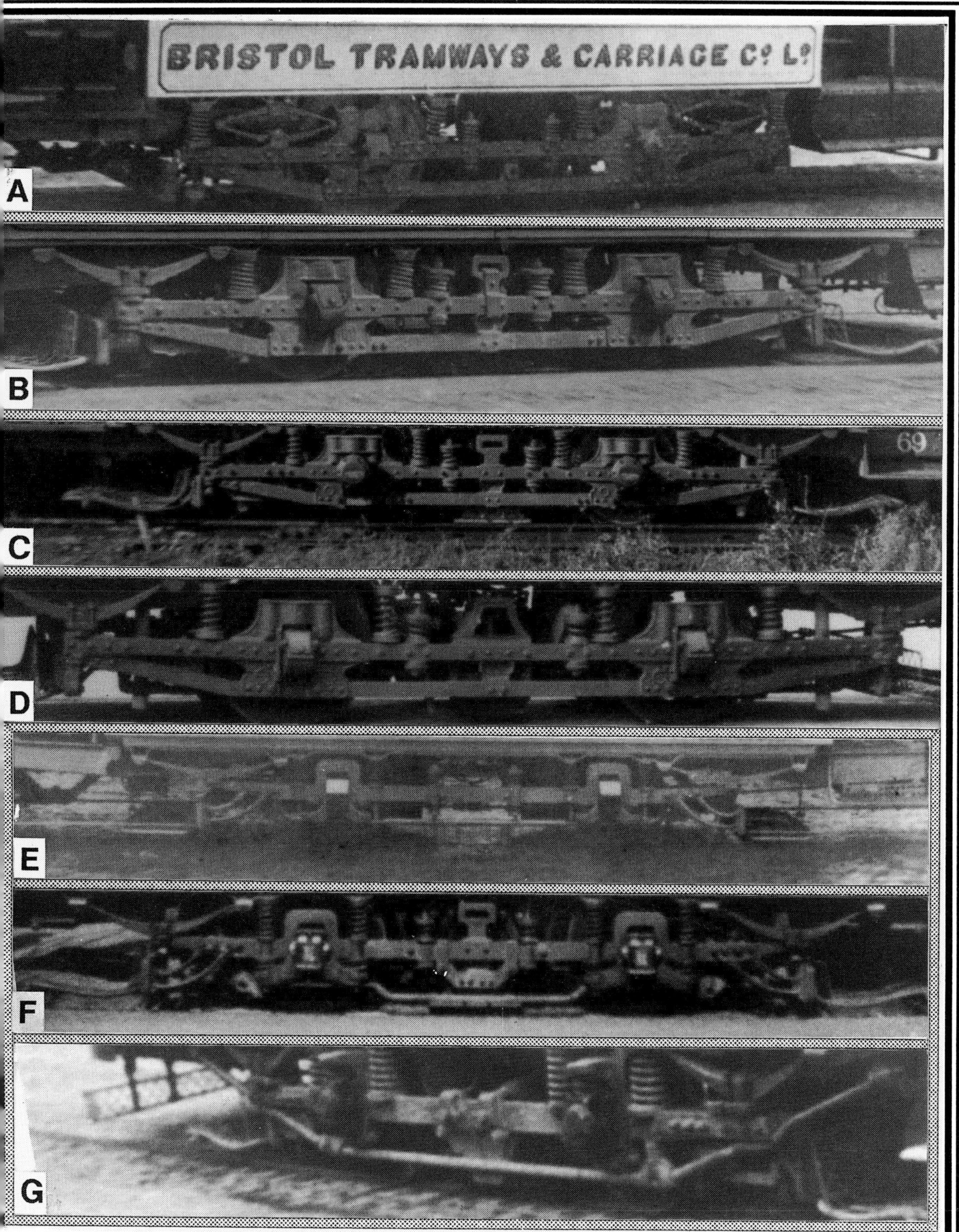

116. Seven different trucks -

A	5ft.6ins.	Peckham Cantilever	Cars 86-97, 116-118 when delivered new.
B	6ft.6ins.	Peckham Cantilever	Majority of fleet, latterly, the Bristol standard truck.
C	6ft.6ins.	Peckham Cantilever	Car 69 with Hoffman Roller Bearings.
D	6ft.6ins.	Peckham Cantilever	Railgrinders 1 and 2
E	6ft.	Brill 21E	Cars 140-161, when delivered new.
F	6ft.6ins.	Brill 21E	Cars 203, 206, 211, 213, 219, 229, latterly.
G	6ft.	McGuire Columbian	Cars 203-232 when delivered new.

Depot allocation

The Company tried to allocate trams in blocks of numbers to each depot and in the main this was kept - some for 40 years!

During 1937/38, my father's notes and those of the late Keith Williams enabled a basis of an allocation list to be created. Fifty years later, having gone through hundreds of photographs, these notes have been extremely useful and the following situation could quite possibly have existed. This is not an official company list.

Horfield	1-13, 37-67, 86, 87, 94, 95, 121, 124, 127, 162, 167, 233-237
Eastville	14-18, 20-25, 27-29, 31-36, 90, 91, 120, 141.
Bedminster	19, 26, 30, 98-112, 119, 125, 128, 136.
Brislington	68-85, 96, 123, 203-232.
Staple Hill	88, 93, 129, 131, 133, 134, 137, 138, 140, 142-149, 151-161, 191, 194.
Kingswood	89, 126, 164, 169-190.
St George	113-115, 118, 122, 130, 132, 135, 139, 150, 163, 165, 166,168, 192, 193, 195-202.

Car Breaking

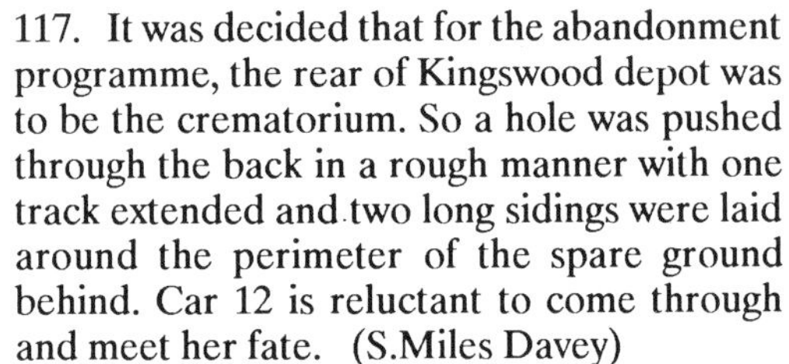

117. It was decided that for the abandonment programme, the rear of Kingswood depot was to be the crematorium. So a hole was pushed through the back in a rough manner with one track extended and two long sidings were laid around the perimeter of the spare ground behind. Car 12 is reluctant to come through and meet her fate. (S.Miles Davey)

118. Trams were lined up for their cremation. The metal went to Habgood's and Pugsley's; the woodwork was burnt here at the rate of six a week. Mr Charles Challenger, Traffic Manager, in 1896, patented the hinged covers on the seats for keeping them dry in wet weather. As the overhead was not on a public highway, it was less than the minimum legal standard of 20ft./6096mm above ground level. (S.Miles Davey)

119. Cars 15 and 51 on death row. Car 51 would be burnt shortly, having had the decency boards already taken away. (S.Miles Davey)

Commencing 9th May 1938, cars were disposed of as follows - 208, 10, 27, 22, 46, 147, 2, 3, 120, 140, 160, 159, 4, 74, 96, 155, 107, 99, 229, 145, 84, 8, 151, 141, 20, 153, 146, 68, 32, 148, 79, 43, 218, 100, 39, 15, 28, 45, 6, 12, 54, 16, 38, 51, 37, Grinder No.2 - 174, 129, 49, 73, 77, 215, 211, 108, 102, 217, 101, 105, 230, 225, 221, 104, 110, 206, 103, 209, 207, 191, 222, 204, 176, 114, 184, 165, 82, 83, 52, 196, 85, 111, 177, 170, 75, 93, 237, 18, 182, 198, 88, 168, 137, 63, 219 (body dismantled, truck retained for spare) 21, 91, 172, 76, 195, 81, 69, 80, 228, 201, 234, 149, 106, 59, 233, 72, 90, 122, and 48.

Commencing 26th June 1939
188, 67, 14, 139, 194, 202, No.3 Plough, 134, 178, 179, 66, 205, 152, 133, 119, 231, 190, 35, 185, 223, 220, 95, 25, 33, 57, 65, 189, 50, 130, 11, 34, 31, 58, 94, 109, 115, 212, 78, 186, 121, 23, 203, 183, 42, 180, 118, 44, 1, 62, 232, and 181.

Commencing 28th January 1941
164, 9, 26, 71, at Bedminster. Then resumed at Kingswood - 89, 227, 236, 128, 98, 226, 56, 55, 24(a), 40, 123, 166, 142, 138(a), 154, 41, 87, 112, 136, 214, 47(a), 210(a), 144(a), 13(a), 125 (changed for 113 which returned to service), and 5. - (a) indicates cars retained on siding since 1939 as "Emergency Reserve."

Commencing 23rd June 1941
124, 29, 19, 161, 156, 17, 60, 235, 127, 30, 163, 162, 131, 143, 199, 70, 192, 132, 197, 167, 150, 113, 175, 86, 126, 135, 216, 213, 157, 187, 36, 7, 173, 171, 224, 193, 53, 169, 61, 200, 158 and 64, which was the last passenger car burned, 16th October 1941. The last cars to be burnt were the two works cars, Grinder No.1 and Plough No.2. This final batch of 44 cars completed the dissolution of a very fine tramway system.

120. The last few minutes of car 205. (S.Miles Davey)

Finale

So now, since 1941, buses rule the roads. Plans never came to fruition for possible extensions to Avonmouth, Downend, Henbury, Keynsham (to connect with Bath's system), Long Ashton, Longwell Green or Warmley.

Sadly no complete Bristol tram exists. Ideas were banded about to build a replica of car 238 on a Peckham truck that was available from a German tramway system.

The only evidence available though is of two bodies from the 98-115 batch of trailers. One (in two halves!) is in the Bristol Industrial Museum together with a quantity of folding top deck seats. The other is in a garden in Downend, Bristol and does at least have sliding doors that open and shut.

In 1939 my father bought destination boards for a penny each when they were being sold off at Kingswood depot. Destination boxes went for one shilling and sixpence (7p) each. These, together with ticket boxes, large enamel advertisement panels, archways over the doors, various signs, the controller handle of car 231, fare charts, time tables and tickets, are now in the author's collection. Only this year I picked up parts of the woodwork of cars 68 and 153 and a pair of sliding doors at a Bristol market!

For over 50 years the Bristol Tram Photograph Collection has grown to hundreds of pictures, photos and post cards from dozens of sources. Except for three trams the whole electric fleet is represented, with most of them in both their original condition and as standard rebuilds. If any reader can supply a picture of cars 79, 97 or 184, a copy would be most welcome.

The system had a very fine safety record. There were only three fatalities out of four serious recorded accidents during its 65 years existence.

121. Six hundred years after Bristol received its 1373 Charter, a massive exhibition was staged on Durdham Downs. The Company had a mock tram body built as their publicity stand. Two of the more attractive staff (Janet Pitt and Irene Barry) are seen decorating "Car 600" on 11th July 1973. (P.G.Davey)

Half a century after the abandonment of the tramways, "the powers that be" have been trying to "re-invent the Bristol tram". If only Brislington could be a tram depot again in (say) 2001, a hundred years after its completion, for Bristol's Metro.

I went there, quite recently. The tracks are down in parts and the last of the huge lamp standards is in store in the old Engineering Shop.

As I walked out through that famous gateway, into Bath Road, I'm sure I heard a bell - two rings - just faintly.